Great Careers

# Personal Care Services, Fitness, and Education

with a High School Diploma

## Titles in the *Great Careers* series

*Great Careers*

# Personal Care Services, Fitness, and Education

*with a High School Diploma*

**Amy Hackney Blackwell**

Ferguson Publishing
*An imprint of Infobase Publishing*

*Great Careers with a High School Diploma*
## Personal Care Services, Fitness, and Education

Ferguson
An imprint of Infobase Publishing
132 West 31st Street
New York, NY 10001

ISBN-13:978-0-8160-7045-9

Library of Congress Cataloging-in-Publication Data

Great careers with a high school diploma. — 1st ed.
    v. cm.
  Includes bibliographical references and index
  Contents: [1] Food, agriculture, and natural resources — [2] Construction and trades — [3] Communications, the arts, and computers —
[4] Sales, marketing, business, and finance — [5] Personal care services, fitness, and education — [6] Health care, medicine, and science —
[7] Hospitality, human services, and tourism — [8] Public safety, law, and security — [9] Manufacturing and transportation — [10] Armed forces.
  ISBN-13: 978-0-8160-7046-6 (v.1)
  ISBN-10: 0-8160-7046-6 (v.1)
  ISBN-13: 978-0-8160-7043-5 (v.2)
  ISBN-10: 0-8160-7043-1 (v.2)
[etc.]
1. Vocational guidance — United States. 2. Occupations — United States.
3. High school graduates — Employment — United States.
  HF5382.5.U5G677 2007
  331.702'330973 — dc22

                                                                2007029883

Ferguson books are available at special discounts when purchased in bulk quantities for businesses, associations, institutions, or sales promotions. Please call our Special Sales Department in New York at (212) 967-8800 or (800) 322-8755.

You can find Ferguson on the World Wide Web at
http://www.fergpubco.com

Produced by Print Matters, Inc.
Text design by A Good Thing, Inc.
Cover design by Salvatore Luongo

Printed in the United States of America

Sheridan PMI 10 9 8 7 6 5 4 3 2 1

This book is printed on acid-free paper.

# Contents

# How to Use This Book

This book, part of the Great Careers with a High School Diploma series, highlights in-demand careers that require no more than a high school diploma or the general educational development (GED) credential and offer opportunities for personal growth and professional advancement to motivated readers who are looking for a field that's right for them. The focus throughout is on the fastest-growing jobs with the best potential for advancement in the field. Readers learn about future prospects while discovering jobs they may never have heard of.

Knowledge—of yourself and about a potential career—is a powerful tool in launching yourself professionally. This book tells you how to use it to your advantage, explore job opportunities, and identify a good fit for yourself in the working world.

Each chapter provides the essential information needed to find not just a job but a career that draws on your particular skills and interests. All chapters include the following features:

- ✴ "Is This Job for You?" presents a set of questions for you to answer about yourself to help you learn if you have what it takes to work in a given career.
- ✴ "Let's Talk Money" and "Lets Talk Trends" provide at a glance crucial information about salary ranges and employment prospects.
- ✴ "What You'll Do" provides descriptions of the essentials of each job.
- ✴ "Where You'll Work" relates the details of the settings and the rules and patterns typical of that field.
- ✴ "Your Typical Day" provides details about what a day on the job involves for each occupation.
- ✴ "The Inside Scoop" presents firsthand information from someone working in the field.
- ✴ "What You Can Do Now" provides advice on getting prepared for your future career.
- ✴ "What Training You'll Need" discusses state requirements, certifications, and courses or other training you may need as you get started on your new career path.
- ✴ "How to Talk Like a Pro" defines a few key terms that give a feel for the occupation.

✴ "How to Find a Job" gives the practical how-tos of landing a position.

✴ "Secrets for Success" and "Reality Check" share inside information on getting ahead.

✴ "Some Other Jobs to Think About" lists similar related careers to consider.

✴ "How You Can Move Up" outlines how people in each occupation turn a job into a career, advancing in responsibility and earnings power.

✴ "Web Sites to Surf" lists Web addresses of trade organizations and other resources providing more information about the career.

In addition to a handy comprehensive index, the back of the book features an appendix providing invaluable information on job hunting strategies and techniques. This section provides general tips on interviewing, constructing a strong résumé, and gathering professional references. Use this book to discover a career that seems right for you—the tools to get you where you want to be are at your fingertips.

# Introduction

For millions of Americans, life after high school means stepping into the real world. Each year, more than 900,000 of the nation's 2.8 million high school graduates go directly into the workforce. Clearly, college isn't for everyone. Many people learn best by using their hands rather than by sitting in a classroom. Others find that the escalating cost of college puts it beyond reach, at least for the time being. During the 2005–2006 school year, for instance, tuition and fees at a four-year public college averaged $5,491, not including housing costs, according to the College Board.

The good news is that there's a wide range of exciting, satisfying careers available without a four-year bachelor's degree or even a two-year associate's degree. Great Careers with a High School Diploma highlights specific in-demand careers in which individuals who have only a high school diploma or credential of general educational development (GED) can find work, with or without further training (outside of college). The training that some of these positions require may be completed either on the job, through a certificate program, or during an apprenticeship, which combines entry-level work and class time.

Happily, there's plenty of growth in the number of jobs that don't require a college diploma. That growth is fastest for positions that call for additional technical training or a certificate of proficiency. The chief economist at the Economic Policy Foundation, a think tank specializing in employment issues, notes that there are simply more of these positions available than there are workers to fill them. In fact, only 23 percent of the jobs available in the coming years will require a four-year degree or higher, the foundation reports.

It's often said that higher education is linked to higher earnings. But this is not the whole story. The gap that exists between the wages of high school graduates and those with college degrees has begun to close slightly. Between 2000 and 2004, the yearly earnings of college graduates dropped by 5.6 percent while the earnings of high school graduates increased modestly by 1.6 percent. High school graduates earn a median yearly income of $26,104, according the U.S. Census Bureau.

So what career should a high school graduate consider? The range is so broad that Great Careers with a High School Diploma includes 10 volumes, each based on related career fields from the Department of Labor's career clusters. Within each volume approximately 10 careers are profiled, so you can focus on a wide selection of job possibilities, some of which you may not even know exist. To enable you to narrow your choices, each chapter offers a self-assessment quiz that helps answer the question, "Is this career for me?" What's more, each job profile includes an insightful look at what the position involves, highlights of a typical day, insight into the work environment, and an interview with someone on that job.

An essential part of the decision to enter a particular field includes how much additional training is needed. Great Careers features opportunities that require no further academic study or training beyond high school as well as those that do. If you're in high school, you can start prepping for a career immediately though volunteer work, internships, academic classes, technical programs, or career academies. (Currently, for instance, one in four high school students concentrate on a vocational or technical program.) For each profile, the best ways to prepare are featured in a "What You Can Do Now" section.

Across the board, employers of entry-level workers aren't looking for degrees and academic achievements. They want employability skills: a sense of responsibility, a willingness to learn, discipline, flexibility, and above all enthusiasm. Luckily, with 100 jobs profiled in Great Careers with a High School Diploma, finding the perfect one to get enthusiastic about is easier than ever.

## *The Varied World of People Services*

This book covers careers in personal care and services, fitness, and education—a broad area with lots of career possibilities. These careers can be great for people who like to work with other people or who like to work with their hands. Personal-care jobs are those jobs that involve care of other peoples' bodies, such as cutting hair, doing facials, tattooing or piercing, or performing spa treatments. The fitness field includes all jobs involving exercise, such as teaching aerobics and yoga or working as a personal trainer. The field of education includes jobs for school aides and preschool aides who work in this field. Service careers also include jobs such as housekeeping and sewing. At the moment the personal care and service sector is a very good place to look for work. Employment in the manufacturing sector, traditionally a good area for high school graduates to look for jobs, has been steadily declining since 2000.

Personal care and service jobs, however, are expected to grow faster than average between now and 2014.

Chapter 1 covers hairstylists and barbers. If hair interests you—if you like to look at pictures of hairstyles and spend hours coloring and styling your own and your friends' hair, or if you just like to see people looking neat and trimmed, then this career might be right for you. There are lots of opportunities available in all types of barbershops and salons, and if you become an expert stylist or colorist you can make a great income. You'll have to get a license and probably spend a couple of years learning your skills, but then you'll be in a growing field where you will meet new people every day. Be ready for competition, though; hair stylist Jet Rhys says of the field, "It's a big industry. You have to be up on your people skills and you have to look sharp."

If you like to spend your time in spas, then definitely check out Chapter 2, which discusses cosmetologists, skin-care specialists, makeup artists, manicurists, and other professionals who spend most of their time touching up and beautifying their clients. The word "cosmetology" can be a little confusing because it can actually covers a wide range of specialties, including hair styling, facials, massage, manicures, makeup, and other spa treatments. Some cosmetologists even end up in laser centers, zapping unwanted hair and wrinkles. If this field interests you, you should read Chapter 1 as well, because there are a lot of similarities between the two career areas. Like hair stylists, cosmetologists have to go to school and get licensed. The training is fastest if you pick just one specialty, such as manicures and pedicures, but you'll make more money if you can provide multiple services. Many cosmetologists specialize in several areas.

Are you an exercise fanatic? Do you spend all your free time in the gym? Do you have a daily yoga practice? Are you a black belt in karate? If so, turn to Chapter 3, which covers careers including fitness instructor, personal trainer, martial arts instructor, and yoga teacher. If you go into the exercise field, you'll get to spend lots of your time engaged in your favorite form of exercise; you'll have to keep in shape for your clients! During your working hours, you'll help clients exercise, either one-on-one or in a group class. You'll watch their form so that they get maximum benefit without hurting themselves. Every body has a unique build and different exercise needs, which is part of the attraction of the field to many practitioners. For example, yoga instructor Paula Lynch says, "There are so many different body types, some students have injuries or disabilities, and even some able-bodied students have more energy or mental blocks. It keeps me learning about the practice in new ways, learning how to apply the asana [pose] practice to specific students' needs." To improve in this profession and to keep up with trends, you'll go to seminars and workshops. This field is especially beneficial for anyone who wants to work evenings and weekends or who might want to work part-time.

Chapter 4 may appeal to you if you're artistic, independent, and like to go your own way. It focuses on tattoo artists and piercing specialists. This chapter discusses the ins and outs of working in the body modification field. The plus side is that the people working in this field seem to really love what they do: They love the artistic side of the work. Tattoo artist Adam Duncan comments, "I like that I can do art all day and all night, all the time." The downside is that this field can be pretty hard to enter, especially if you want to be a tattoo artist. Almost all tattoo artists have to go through an apprenticeship, which can take years and costs thousands of dollars. Once they finish their training, though, they can spend the rest of their lives decorating peoples' bodies with permanent drawings and body jewelry.

Do you like babies and toddlers? Do you find little kids irresistible? Then check out Chapter 5, which is on nannies, babysitters, and day care assistants. If you go into this field, you'll spend your workdays taking care of little tykes, from the tiniest newborns to kids nearly ready for kindergarten. If you work as a nanny or babysitter, you may also work with older kids after school, on weekends, and during vacations. You'll change diapers, sing lullabies, serve snacks, and clean up spills. You'll need endless patience, but your reward will be lots of little hugs and smiles.

Chapter 6 is about preschool aides and school aides. If you like working with kids but like them a bit older than babies and toddlers, you might enjoy this field. Schools of all levels need aides and assistants to help the main teachers with their daily work. As an aide you may greet kids in the morning, prepare materials for them to use in class, help them get lunch, and watch them at recess. This is a great field for anyone who wants to make a real difference in a child's life. This career is also a good stepping-stone for those who might want to become a teacher later on.

Are you a clean freak? Do you like to make a house neat and tidy? Chapter 7 would interest you—it's about housekeepers, maids, janitors, and other cleaners. This field employs a huge number of people; in 2004, over 4 million people were working as cleaners, so there are always tons of jobs available. There are all sorts of cleaning jobs, too.

You could work for a hotel, a hospital, or a school, or you could clean houses. This field is very easy to enter; you won't need any extra training as long as you're enthusiastic, strong, and can do the work.

You may never have considered a career as a funeral attendant, but you might after reading Chapter 8. People die every day, so there's a steady need for funeral workers. Funeral attendants do all kinds of jobs, from polishing limousines to collecting dead bodies from the morgue. You'll have to be neat, polite, and punctual—and be interested, rather than turned off, by human biology and the idea of dead bodies—if you want to succeed in this field. Funeral attendants insist that their job isn't at all grim or ghoulish. Funeral attendant Randy Clark says when he is helping to embalm a dead body, "I always like to think of the person being someone I love and care about." He adds that showing proper respect and care for the bereaved is another meaningful part of his job.

Chapter 9 covers floral designers. This is a wonderful field for anyone who likes flowers and has artistic ambitions. Floral designer Holly Kromer especially likes that "every day I get to do different designs with different flower choices and colors." Floral design is also a great field for people who enjoy weddings, proms, and other parties. Of course, floral arrangements are also a part of sad occasions such as funerals. Depending on where you work, you may spend all your time arranging flowers or you may do a variety of tasks, including helping customers choose arrangements and driving a van to deliver and set up flowers at events. To become a floral designer, you'll probably want to go to school for at least a few weeks or months so you can learn all the necessary tricks of the trade.

If you know how to sew and like it, you should consider a career as a seamstress, tailor, or upholsterer, discussed in Chapter 10. In these jobs you would measure people or furniture and cut and sew cloth to fit them precisely. All sewing careers are fairly difficult, and it takes several years to master these trades. But if you know the basics and are willing to learn, you can get a job doing simple sewing and gradually work your way up to a master craftsperson.

Most of these fields are not hard to enter, though many of them take years to master. Many of these jobs are deeply satisfying to their practitioners. Personal service jobs offer the chance to make a real difference in someone's life, whether it be by caring for toddlers, giving a fabulous massage, letting a grieving spouse cry on your shoulder at a funeral, or running a great exercise class. In these fields you can often see the results of your work immediately, such as when you clean a filthy house or sew a perfect garment. If you have artistic ambitions, many of these fields offer numerous creative opportunities, from creating tattoo designs to dying a client's hair the perfect shade of red. And many personal service, fitness, and education jobs are great for anyone who wants a flexible schedule or would prefer to work part time. There are jobs in this area that could suit you—whether you're a people person or an introvert.

Opportunities in personal care and services, fitness, and education include some of the most plentiful and popular jobs in the country. If you think you'd like to help people, work with your hands, be creative in your work, or spend your days doing your favorite exercise, you should consider one of the careers profiled in this chapter.

*Make your customers look great*

# Hairstylist, Barber

*Perform a vital service*

*Keep up with the latest hair trends*

# Hairstylist, Barber

Hairstylists and barbers take care of people's hair. They style, cut, shampoo and condition, color, highlight, fit hairpieces, blow-dry, and arrange hair for special occasions. Today more than 300,000 people work as barbers and hairdressers, and exciting opportunities exist for anyone who wants to dedicate themselves to mastering the latest hair trends. Of course, the competition at the best salons is intense, and styles change continually, from Jennifer Aniston's layered "Rachel" 1990s cut to Jessica Alba's recent wavy look. Beyond the creativity, cutting and styling hair is a great profession for anyone who likes to meet people, make customers feel great, and work a flexible schedule. You'll need to spend at least a few months training at a beauty or salon school and get a state license. Then you can be on your way to make your customers look fabulous.

## Is This Job for You?

Answer the following questions to see whether a career as a barber or hairstylist is right for you.

| | | | |
|---|---|---|---|
| *Yes* | *No* | **1.** | Are you fascinated by hairstyles? |
| *Yes* | *No* | **2.** | Do you like to meet different people every day? |
| *Yes* | *No* | **3.** | Can you work on your feet for hours? |
| *Yes* | *No* | **4.** | Do you like to work with your hands? |
| *Yes* | *No* | **5.** | Do you enjoy studying magazine fashion and hair trends? |
| *Yes* | *No* | **6.** | Can you work well with other people? |
| *Yes* | *No* | **7.** | Are you good at handling complaints and criticism? |
| *Yes* | *No* | **8.** | Can you keep your work area neat and your tools sterile? |
| *Yes* | *No* | **9.** | Are you good at listening to and following directions? |
| *Yes* | *No* | **10.** | Do you feel comfortable working weekends and evenings? |

If you answered "Yes" to most of these questions, you may have what it take to be a hairstylist or barber. To find out more about these professions, read on.

## *Let's Talk Money*

Hairstylists and barbers make an average income of about $24,000, according to 2006 data from the U.S. Bureau of Labor Statistics. Some high-end hairstylists earn quite a bit more; the top hairdressers pull in over $40,000. Shampooers average $16,320.

## *What You'll Do*

Barbers and hairstylists do basically the same work, but barbers tend to be male and serve a male clientele in basic surroundings. Hairstylists (either male or female) serve men and women and often create more elaborate cuts. Either way, you'll spend a lot of time in your client's hair. You'll start by discussing the cut a client wants, perhaps looking at photos he or she has selected from magazines. You'll also evaluate the shape of your client's face and the texture of his or her hair so you can use the proper cutting techniques. In some salons, you may shampoo and condition your client's hair. In others, a shampooer or assistant will do it. Once the client is in your chair, wearing a salon robe or draped, you'll carefully trim or cut his or her hair using precise techniques as well as your own creative talents to give your client the look he or she wants.

While you cut, you may also get to know your client or catch up. Your personal connection with your customers is essential to keeping them happy and turning them into steady customers. If you're cutting off several inches or more, you may suggest that your client donate the cut hair to Locks of Love. If your client requests hair color, such as highlights, or a chemical straightening process, you'll do the work before or after the cut, depending on what has been asked for. In most salons, you'll also blow dry your client's hair. You may also recommend a product or two; commission on these sales may be an important part of your wages. Throughout the appointment, your expertise is essential to your customer's satisfaction.

If you're a barber, your work will be similar, though more straightforward. However, your customers may also ask for help in concealing full or partial hair loss, perhaps with a hairpiece. You may also trim beards, color hair, shave client's faces, and perform simple facials. You'll sterilize your equipment and scissors, and

## Let's Talk Trends

About half of all barbers and hairstylists are self-employed. Flexible schedules are common. Job opportunities are plentiful, but the best jobs are hard to get. If you're trained and licensed to provide multiple services, such as specialty cuts and coloring techniques, color correction, extensions, or special occasion hairstyles, you'll be able to find better jobs and earn more money.

keep your scissors are sharp. Whether you're a barber or a stylist, do your job well, and you'll be on your way to building a base of steady clients.

## *Who* You'll Work For

* ✶ A barbershop
* ✶ An owner-operated salon
* ✶ A salon that's part of a chain
* ✶ A spa
* ✶ Yourself

## *Where* You'll Work

Barbershops are typically utilitarian establishments. Some still have the traditional red-and-white striped barber pole out front. A barbershop may have several chairs all in a row next to each other facing a mirror. It will contain one or more sinks for shampooing customers, though not all barbershop customers want a shampoo.

A salon is usually more luxuriously decorated than a barbershop. The shampoo sinks may be in their own room. The chairs may be more separated than the ones in a barbershop to give clients more of a sense of privacy, though this isn't always the case. There will be changing rooms for clients who need to put on smocks before color treatments or perms. You'll spend some of your time around harsh chemicals, so you'll need to wear protective gloves and a smock.

Hair salons often offer services besides haircuts and treatments, and there may be a separate work area for manicurists, facialists, or

# The Inside Scoop: Q&A

**Jet Rhys**
**Hairstylist and business owner**
**San Diego, California**

**Q:** *How did you get your job?*

**A:** When I was six years old I knew I wanted to do this. My parents wanted me to go to college, but I didn't want to. In my junior and senior years, I worked on my academic credits for a half day and took beauty school classes in the afternoon. When I finished my senior year, I received my high school diploma and my cosmetology diploma. Then I got an internship at Vidal Sassoon for 15 months, where I swept up, cleaned the bathroom, and brought in my own models to work on, all for minimum wage. Now I have my own hair salon.

**Q:** *What do you like best about your job?*

**A:** Being in a service industry and knowing that I have the proper training behind me, and the self-confidence to do the job well. You're serving people and you're making them feel good about themselves. You have such confidence when you're trained. You feel like, "I can do this, I can make this person over, I can fix this hair challenge."

**Q:** *What's the most challenging part of your job?*

**A:** Learning that you're not going to make everybody happy. You may think one way and they may think another. Communication with a client is the most challenging part of my job.

**Q:** *What are the keys to success to being a hairstylist?*

**A:** Staying current. You have to be well trained and you have to have positive energy. You have to have great listening skills, you have to sell yourself and your ideas, you have to be great at what you do, and you have to treat that client that's been coming to you for 10 years like it's the first time, every time.

makeup artists. You may find a hairstyling job at a spa, which will contain facilities for massages and other spa treatments. Barbershops and hair salons can be found in every location from a strip mall or shopping mall to a Victorian-style home on the main street of a small town to a corporate office building.

## *Your Typical Day*

Here are some highlights of a typical day for a hairstylist.

✔ **Give someone highlights and a cut.** You spend an hour carefully gathering small sections of a customer's hair. You paint them with a bleach solution, wrap them with foil, set a timer, and settle your client under a heat lamp. While her hair lightens, you cut your next customer's hair. When the timer buzzes, you remove the foils, wash, trim, and blow-dry your client's hair. She leaves you a generous tip.

✔ **Whip up a wedding up-do.** A bride arrives with her sister three hours before her wedding. You sweep up her hair into an up-do of gentle curls, fasten her veil, and carefully pull out a few wisps to match the photo she's brought you.

✔ **Next comes the wind-down.** After several more hair appointments, and dealing with one customer's complaint, you clean your station, sterilize your brushes, and check your supply of styling products to get ready for your next day.

## *What You Can Do Now*

✴ Take hairstyling classes at high school.
✴ Study at pictures of hairstyles in magazines and on TV.
✴ Get a job shampooing hair or cleaning up at a local salon.
✴ Practice the techniques you learn on your friends and family members.

## *What Training You'll Need*

You'll have to get a license before you can work as a barber or hairstylist. What you'll have to do to get this license depends on your state. In most states you have to be at least 16 years old and have graduated from a state-licensed cosmetology or barber school. Some states require you to have a high school diploma. In others, finishing eighth grade is enough. To get a license, you have to pass a written test and demonstrate that you can cut hair, create certain hairstyles, sterilize and sharpen your equipment, and handle coloring and perm chemicals properly. If you move to another state, you'll have to get licensed again.

Though some vocational high schools offer courses in hairstyling, most people do their pre-license training at beauty school (also called hair or salon school) or barber school. You should check the school's course offerings to make sure it teaches exactly what you want to learn. To become a hairstylist or barber, you'll need to take courses in cutting hair, coloring hair, hairstyling, and health and safety. You could spend anywhere from several months up to two years taking classes. How long school takes often depends on how much time you can put in. Once you've graduated, you may have to work as an apprentice in a beauty salon or barbershop for a few months to more than a year. During this time, you'll perform clean up duties and watch senior stylists work. You'll also practice your hairstyling skills, starting off with the simplest techniques and gradually working up to more difficult cuts and styles. Many stylists like to take continuing education courses to keep their skills sharp and current.

## *How to Talk Like a Pro*

Here are a few words you'll hear as a hairstylist or barber:

- ✴ **Extensions** Pieces of hair attached to a person's natural hair in order to make the hair appear longer; extensions can be attached with glue or metal rings or by braiding or weaving in the extension.
- ✴ **French twist** A hairstyle in which a woman's hair is twisted in a vertical roll and pinned at the back of her head.
- ✴ **Highlights** Light streaks in hair made by bleaching selected strands.
- ✴ **Lowlights** Dark streaks in hair made by dyeing selected strands.
- ✴ **Toupee** A term older men may use to refer to a hairpiece or partial wig worn to cover a bald spot.

# *How to Find a Job*

To find a job as a hairstylist or barber, start with your high school or cosmetology school's placement service. Some salons will place advertisements for workers in newspapers, on school bulletin boards, or online. If you really want to be good at what you do, you'll probably want to complete an internship at a major salon or hairstyling company. These internships can be very competitive, and it can take months of persistence to land one. If at first you don't succeed, call back every month or so. Send cards on holidays so that the company will remember you. When you get an interview, practice what you're going to say with family and friends before you go to the salon. When you go to the interview, look sharp and show up on time; one of the biggest problems in the beauty industry are employees who fail to show up when they're scheduled. Tell the interviewer you want to be part of a team and work in a learning environment and that you'll do whatever it takes to be a great hairstylist.

You can also start building up your client base by working as a freelance stylist out of your home or apartment, offering cuts to friends and family members for a reasonable fee. If you're good they may rely on you. Then when you apply for a salon job, you may be ahead of the competition if you can demonstrate that you have your own "following" of customers.

# *Secrets for Success*

See the following suggestions and turn to the appendix for advice on résumés and interviews.

✦ Do your best to make your customers happy. The best source of new business is word of mouth, and the best clients are the ones who keep coming back because they love your work and can't imagine letting anyone else cut their hair. Customers tend to become extremely loyal to individual stylists.

✦ There are many different kinds of barbershops and salons; apprenticeship is a good opportunity find the sort of establishment that is right for you.

# *Reality Check*

Many salons pay their stylists on commission, not a salary. If you're paid on commission, the more regular clients you have, the more money you'll make. You may have to act like a salesperson, pushing clients to buy more services and products.

## Some Other Jobs to Think About

* Shampooer. You won't need any formal training or a license to get started washing and conditioning hair.
* Stylist specializing in weaves and extensions. You'll study techniques that will enable you to create elaborate looks—especially braided styles, with real hair or extensions.
* Cosmetologist. You'll do facials, manicures, spa treatments, and makeup.

## How You Can Move Up

* Open your own salon or barbershop. If you run your own business, you'll take the lion's share of the profits. You'll also get to decide how to decorate, what products to carry, and who will work for you. To succeed, take courses in management, marketing, and business basics.
* Learn specialties. Hairstylists who can provide lots of different services make more money than those who just cut hair. Become a colorist or an expert in color correction. (Women will pay big bucks for stylists who can fix their home-coloring disasters.) Master the latest specialty hair cutting techniques.

### Web Sites to Surf

**Careers in Beauty.** This site offers information on careers in hairstyling and cosmetology. It also details grants and scholarships and schools throughout the country. It's associated with the American Association of Cosmetology Schools (AACS).  http://www.careersinbeauty.org

**Professional Beauty Association.** This association provides various services for beauty professionals, including advocacy, business help, and training. http://www.probeauty.org

**Makeup Alley.** Members contribute reviews of hair and beauty products and discuss hair care and other cosmetics topics. http://www.makeupalley.com

*Work in a soothing environment*

# Cosmetologist, Skin-care Specialist, Makeup Artist, Manicurist

*Beautify and improve faces, skin, and nails*

*Make customers look and feel great*

# Cosmetologist, *Skin-care Specialist, Makeup Artist, Manicurist*

Do you have a long-standing interest in makeup and nail polish? Would you happily spend your weekends in a spa? Do you have a knack for knowing how to make your friends look and feel good? Are you fascinated by the details of skin care products and regimes? You may be a natural cosmetologist. Cosmetology includes many specialties, including hairstyling, skin care, makeup, manicures, waxing, and more. In fact, it's an ancient career. Ever since Cleopatra lined her eyes in black and the Greeks relaxed in fragrant baths, men and women have specialized in adorning, beautifying, and treating the face and body. Today cosmetology is a fast-growing field with plenty of opportunities. What's more, although cosmetologists can spend years learning their craft, you can enter the field after a few months of training.

## Is This Job for You?

To find out if being a cosmetologist is right for you, read each of the following questions and answer "Yes" or "No."

Yes   No   **1.** Do you like to work with your hands?

Yes   No   **2.** Are you comfortable having physical contact with people?

Yes   No   **3.** Can you stand on your feet for eight hours a day?

Yes   No   **4.** Are you careful and detail-oriented?

Yes   No   **5.** Do you listen and follow directions well?

Yes   No   **6.** Can you keep your work area clean and your tools sterilized?

Yes   No   **7.** Are you good at handling criticism?

Yes   No   **8.** Do you enjoy meeting new people every day?

Yes   No   **9.** Are you good at managing time and keeping to a schedule?

Yes   No   **10.** Are you interested in skincare and personal grooming?

If you answered "Yes" to most of these questions, you may have the talent to pursue a career as a cosmetologist. To find out more about this job, read on.

## Let's Talk Money

In 2005, the average cosmetologist earned about $23,600 a year, or about $11 per hour. Manicurists and pedicurists made slightly less than $10 an hour on average, giving them a yearly income of $20,400. Makeup artists averaged $32,660 a year, and skin-care specialists averaged $26,830.

## What You'll Do

The term "cosmetologist" is really a catch-all word for anyone who works on appearances—doing hair, makeup, skin care, or nails. Some cosmetologists specialize in one or two areas, while others perform a range of different types of services. If you become a cosmetologist, you could specialize in haircuts, hair coloring, hair straightening or perms—all the things that hairstylists do. You might also do facials, hair removal, simple massage techniques, or run tanning beds. You might be trained in manicures and pedicures. You might specialize in applying makeup. As a certified cosmetologist, you can have your pick of jobs.

Many spas now offer treatments such as oxygen facials or seaweed wraps. Some cosmetology programs provide training in these techniques. As a manicurist or pedicurist, you'll take care of fingernails and toenails. You'll file nails, trim cuticles, apply lotion to hands and feet, and polish nails in the latest colors. Some of your clients will want nail extensions. You'll have to be careful to keep your tools and water sterile so you don't spread diseases among your clients. As a skin-care specialist or esthetician, you'll perform facials. You'll look through a magnifying lens to scrutinize pores and extract blackheads. You'll apply chemical peels and perform microdermabrasions. You'll apply cleansers, toners, and moisturizers to the skin, often using special motions as you add and wipe off the products. You may remove unwanted hair with wax, tweezers, or other techniques. Some estheticians specialize in laser treatments, removing hair, treating cellulite, and doing skin rejuvenations. You'll talk with your clients about their needs and recommend skin-care products to them.

As a makeup artist, you'll learn how colors, glosses, powders, and liquid makeup work together to achieve daytime and evening looks for your clients. You'll learn the properties of many brands of makeup. You may work with clients who are on their way to special functions, such as proms or weddings. You may work in a theater or for a film studio.

## *Who* You'll Work For

* A manicure/pedicure shop
* A beauty salon
* A department store
* A day spa or destination spa
* A specialty laser clinic
* A theater
* A film studio

## *Where* You'll Work

Most cosmetologists work in beauty salons, spas, or manicure shops. If you become a laser technician, you could work in a laser treatment center or a dermatologist's office. If you work in a salon, you'll spend your time around shampoo sinks, mirrors, and hairstyling equipment and supplies. You might do much of your work in a large room with several other employees and customers. You'll have to be polite and presentable at all times. Nail salons are often arranged in a similar way. Smells can be very strong in hair salons or manicure shops. You'll have to be careful when handling hair dyes, hair straightening solutions, and nail polishes.

Some cosmetic treatments are done behind closed doors—clients may be naked or nearly naked for body waxes, tanning, and other

## *Let's Talk Trends*

Demand for cosmetic workers is high and expected to increase as salon services gain in popularity and the number of day spas increases. Turnover in the field is also high, keeping up demand for employees. The U.S. Bureau of Labor Statistics predicts that employment among manicurists and skin-care specialists will grow faster than average between now and 2014. Competition is fierce for the best-paying jobs at the most prestigious salons and spas.

body treatments, and it will be your job to protect their privacy. If you work with a laser, you'll have to remember to use eye protection so you don't burn your eyes.

As a makeup artist, you may work in a salon or a spa, preparing women for special occasions such as proms, weddings, or photo shoots. Some makeup artists work at theaters or film studios, getting actors ready for their appearances.

# *Your* Typical Day

Here are the highlights of a typical day for a cosmetologist at a hair, nail, and tanning salon.

✓ **Make those tips tip-top.** You arrive at work at 8:30 a.m. with three manicures on your schedule. You carefully sterilize your equipment after each client by immersing your tools in disinfectant; you throw away anything that can't be disinfected, including emery boards and orange sticks.

✓ **Set up for tanning.** Your salon has two tanning beds in a back room. Two customers come to tan during their lunch break. You greet them, set them up in the tanning beds, carefully setting the lamps based in part on eachyour client's skin type.

✓ **Make up the bride.** You apply makeup to a bride for her evening wedding after your colleague arranges her hair. You go for the latest wedding look—a polished yet naturally dramatic effect. After your long day, you help clean the spa, check your supplies and make a note to order new products.

# *What* You Can Do Now

✯ Take high school cosmetology classes.
✯ Read articles about skin care and hairstyles.
✯ Practice doing your own face, facials, and nails. You can also practice on family and friends.
✯ Read up on different types of skin care products and ingredients and what they do.

# *What* Training You'll Need

Whatever specialty you choose, you'll need to spend at least three months going to cosmetology school. A general program in cosmetology

# The Inside Scoop: Q&A

**Meghann Lawrence**
**Spa specialist**
**Seattle, Washington**

**Q:** *How did you get your job?*

**A:** I moved from California back to Washington and was having a hard time finding a spa in Seattle to work in. A girlfriend of mine was familiar with Ummelin. She wrote a letter of recommendation for me and I dropped off my résumé there.

**Q:** *What do you like best about your job?*

**A:** It gives me freedom to move from city to city, state to state, even country to country. I was very interested in moving around and experiencing different areas, and I was able to do this with my career decision. There are so many things to learn as far as continuing education. Also, it only took me one year to become licensed.

**Q:** *What's the most challenging part of your job?*

**A:** This job can be physically demanding on your body. You want to give so much to your clients, and they often need a lot of compassion and extra attention. I have found that people in this industry are healers and very giving. So at times it's easy to give too much of your energy to one person.

**Q:** *What are the keys to success to being a spa specialist?*

**A:** Technical skills [see "What Training You'll Need" for some examples of skills], good communication skills, being flexible, getting as much education in your field as possible, and having the passion to work with people and help them.

will train you to do a variety of jobs. You'll study hair styling, hair coloring, makeup, skin care, and nail care. A full degree program in cosmetology can take two years or so; the required number of hours of education varies by state. You can also specialize in one area of cosmetics treatment, such as skin or nails. If you do this, your training could be much shorter than if you study all aspects of cosmetology; for example, a manicurist can be certified in just three or four months. Whatever your specialty, you'll have to get licensed in your state. You'll have to prove that you've taken the required number of hours of class time and then take a written and practical test to prove that you know the essential skills for your job.

As an esthetician or skin-care specialist, you'll have to learn all about skin. You'll learn how to identify skin conditions, clean pores, extract blackheads, and massage skin to improve circulation. You'll practice doing chemical peels, eyebrow shaping, and waxing. You may take training in corrective makeup so that you can help people who have had skin surgery or laser treatments look better while they recover.

If you become a manicurist or pedicurist, you'll have to take a training course in nail health and maintenance. You'll practice treating nails and cuticles, shaping nails into attractive shapes, polishing nails, applying artificial nails or nail wraps, and nail art.

If you specialize in laser treatments, you'll have to take training courses on the particular lasers you'll be using. You'll practice assessing people's skin types, choosing laser settings that won't burn your clients, removing hair, doing facial rejuvenation, and post-laser skin treatment. Many cosmetologists take regular continuing education courses to keep up with trends in their fields and to learn new specialties. Clients will want the latest techniques and products in facials, hair removal, makeup, and spa treatment, so you may want to study aromatherapy, thalassotherapy (seawater treatments), specialty facial peels, herbal therapy, essential oil treatment, ear candling, body sugaring, nutrition, sun protection, mineral makeup artistry, or any number of other techniques.

## *How to Talk Like a Pro*

Here are few terms you may hear in cosmetology work:

- ✦ **Electrolysis** A method of removing hair permanently by applying electricity to hair follicles.
- ✦ **Esthetics** The study of skin care, facials, cosmetics, waxing, and other areas, such as massage or reflexology.
- ✦ **Hot stone therapy** The process of placing hot stones on a customer's body to release tension.

✴ **Reflexology** The practice of stimulating pressure points on the feet to affect other parts of the body.

# How to Find a Job

There are lots of jobs available for cosmetologists and personal appearance workers. Many cosmetology schools will offer some service to help graduates find a position, and cosmetology businesses often contact schools if they need new employees. (A good placement service is one thing to look for in your training program.) You can also look for ads in the newspaper or online; do an Internet search for "cosmetologist" plus your hometown.

Word of mouth and connections are the best ways to find jobs. If you have friends who work in the field, ask them about job openings. You can visit salons and spas in person and tell them you're a certified worker looking for a job. The best salons have many job applicants, and it can take a long time to land a job at a prestigious salon. Successful cosmetologists recommend extreme persistence if you want a job at a top spa; call the manager every month to see if they have any openings, describe your skills and interests, send holiday cards, and be flexible about what position you're willing to take.

If you get an interview, conduct a trial run with a friend before you go. Be sure to show up on time and be polite. Your prospective employer will want to know that you're reliable and will treat customers well. Try to look great yourself. If a salon offers you lousy hours or a job that's not your first choice, consider accepting the job anyway. You can always adjust your schedule or specialty after you've worked there for a few months.

# Secrets for Success

See the following suggestions and turn to the appendix for advice on résumés and interviews.

✴ Cosmetologists work with a great variety of customers. Some will want to have conversations while you work, and others will want to stay silent. If your client wants to talk, be sure you're a good listener; don't do most of the talking yourself!

✴ Remember, the looks you help someone create may not be lasting, but the experiences they have while all dolled up may stay with them.

# Reality *Check*

Are you a good salesperson? Many spas expect their employees to sell products such as shampoo or makeup to customers. The cosmetologists who make the most money are often the ones who are also good at integrating sales pitches into treatment sessions.

# Some *Other Jobs to Think About*

*   Hairstylist. If hair is your passion, you can specialize in cutting, styling, and treating hair.
*   Massage therapist. If you like to work in a more physical way, consider becoming a certified massage therapist. At a massage therapy school, you'll learn anatomy and techniques for releasing tension.
*   Cosmetic product salesperson. Cosmetics companies always need representatives to show off their products. You could travel to different salons selling shampoo and lotions and you'd get free samples.
*   Tattoo artist or piercing specialist. Makeup and haircuts not permanent enough for you? Tattoo artists and piercers also get to enhance their customers' looks—for keeps!

# How *You Can Move Up*

*   Specialize. Cosmetologists who can perform specialty treatments such as complicated facials and who keep up with the trends get the best jobs at the best salons and spas. They also earn the best salaries and receive the highest tips. Similarly, become licensed in massage therapy. If you can perform facials and massages at a spa, you'll be in high demand.
*   Open your own salon or day spa. If you have a good head for business, you could aim to open your own beauty business. As an entrepreneur, you can offer your choice of treatments, each customized to reflect your own tastes and beliefs. You can set your own prices and take a percentage of your employees' earnings.

## Web Sites to Surf

**National Cosmetology Association** The NCA is the world's largest association of salon professionals. It has about 25,000 members, including estheticians, nail technicians, hairdressers, salon owners, teachers, and students. http://www.ncacares.org

**Beauty Schools Directory** This Web site can help you choose a school and a program of study.  http://www.beautyschoolsdirectory.com

Join a fast-growing field

# Fitness Instructor

Help people shape up, lose weight

Promote inner balance and peace

# *Fitness Instructor*

Fitness workers help people exercise and move their bodies. They may work one-on-one with clients, customizing workouts for each customer, or they may teach large classes. Fitness workers oversee all sorts of movement and exercise techniques, including weightlifting, spinning, Pilates, yoga, and martial arts. The trends in fitness change constantly, so professionals must keep up-to-date. What's more, within many specialties, such as yoga, there are dozens of schools of techniques among which to choose.

In 2005, 190,000 people worked as fitness instructors in the United States. These numbers hardly capture the excitement and growth of many of these fitness specialties. American consumers, for example, spent more than $2 billion on yoga-related classes and products in 2006, and the trend is up dramatically over the past few years. Interest in fitness is expected to continue to rise as Americans become increasingly health-conscious and interested in losing weight, staying flexible, and keeping toned. Exercise and fitness is a great field for someone with lots of energy and good people skills; it's also great for someone who wants a flexible schedule.

## *Is This Job for You?*

| Yes | No | | |
|-----|----|----|----|
| Yes | No | **1.** | Do you enjoy physical activity? |
| Yes | No | **2.** | Do you enjoy helping other people stay fit? |
| Yes | No | **3.** | Do you enjoy learning about physical fitness and anatomy? |
| Yes | No | **4.** | Are you patient? |
| Yes | No | **5.** | Are you energetic? |
| Yes | No | **6.** | Could you work evenings, weekends, or early mornings? |
| Yes | No | **7.** | Are you organized and reliable? |
| Yes | No | **8.** | Are you outgoing and willing to talk to strangers? |
| Yes | No | **9.** | Can you keep up with changing fitness trends? |
| Yes | No | **10.** | Are you healthy and strong? |

If you answered "Yes" to most of these questions, you may have the talent to pursue a career in fitness. To find out more about this profession, read on.

## Let's Talk Money

The median income for fitness trainers and aerobics instructors is $31,060, according to 2006 data from the U.S. Bureau of Labor Statistics. Many fitness workers work part-time for about $15 an hour, which, if they worked full-time, would equal about $30,000 a year.

## What You'll Do

Fitness workers help people exercise and take part in fitness routines, such as yoga. If you go into the fitness field, you may find yourself working with classes or individuals, putting them through their paces. Fitness instructors teach classes in any number of other activities that go in and out of fashion. If you work as a fitness instructor, you'll plan group classes that are fun and strenuous, but not too difficult. You may choose music to play during the class to increase your students' motivation. You'll demonstrate moves and then make sure the participants do them correctly so that they don't get hurt. You'll be a combination drill sergeant and cheerleader, encouraging everyone to work hard.

Personal trainers work one-on-one with clients, customizing workouts to their clients' individual wants and needs. As a personal trainer, you may work with clients at a gym or in their homes. You'll actually stand over your clients as they exercise, encouraging them to heights of performance. You'll track their progress and adjust the exercises as they get stronger.

## Let's Talk Trends

The fitness industry is growing rapidly because people are increasingly concerned about optimizing their weight and gaining the physical and mental benefits of exercise. The Bureau of Labor Statistics predicts that people will spend increasing amounts on fitness services in the next 10 years as health concerns grow among aging baby boomers, parents put their children in health clubs to combat childhood obesity, and businesses implement health and fitness programs. The job outlook for this field is terrific—employment in the fitness field is expected to increase 27 percent or more by 2014.

As a yoga instructor, you may lead classes in yoga techniques as well as teach private students. You may specialize in a particular style of yoga, such as Ashtanga or Iyengar, or you may create classes that blend styles. You'll call out poses and demonstrate them. You'll help your students maintain correct breathing with their poses and you'll lead them in a meditation or relaxation exercise at the end of class.

As a martial arts instructor, you'll teach adults and children martial arts techniques such as karate or aikido. You'll demonstrate all moves for your students and oversee their exercises and routines. You'll give occasional tests to see if your students have mastered enough skills to earn new belts.

## *Who* You'll Work For

* Gyms and health clubs
* Yoga studios
* Martial arts schools
* Corporations with exercise programs
* Destination resort spas
* Yourself

## *Where* You'll Work

There are jobs for fitness instructors in all sorts of venues, including some you'd never expect. You could work anywhere from a health club to a fancy resort. Most fitness professionals work in gyms and health clubs. If you can teach classes such as aqua fitness, step aerobics, gyrotonics, or another kind of fitness class, you should be able to find a job at a health club. You may find jobs at several different health clubs; it's common for fitness instructors to teach at more than one location every week, especially if they work for a health club that has several branches in one city. Yoga teachers, martial arts instructors, Pilates teachers, and other specialized instructors can work at general health clubs or at specialized studios.

Health clubs aren't the only employers that will want to hire you. Corporations, rehabilitation centers, cruise ships, luxury spas, and island resorts all need fitness instructors and trainers to work with employees or guests. If you like visiting people in their homes, personal training might be a great option for you. Personal trainers often make house calls to motivate and train time-squeezed clients. Fitness work can also be a great career if you want to work at home—if you become a personal trainer, yoga instructor, or Pilates teacher, you can have your clients visit you in your own home studio.

# Your Typical Day

Here are the highlights of a typical day for a fitness instructor.

✓ **Get up and go.** You have to teach two pre-work aerobics class at a health club. You get up at 5:30 a.m. and get to the club by 6:20 a.m. to get ready for your 6:30 a.m. class.

✓ **Make the morning rounds.** You spend the morning circulating in the health club's weight room, helping clients choose weights and correcting their weight-lifting technique. You finish at noon.

✓ **Teach yoga in the evening.** At 6 p.m. you teach a yoga class at a downtown yoga studio. You arrive at the studio at 5:50 p.m. to start your music and set up your mat. Class ends at 7:30 p.m., and your workday is over. You go to bed early so you can get up for the early aerobics class tomorrow.

# What You Can Do Now

✴ Try a variety of styles of exercise, including weight training, aerobics, other health club classes, martial arts, running, or whatever else appeals to you. When you know what you like, you may decide to specialize.

✴ Work out at the gym, lift weights, run, and ride bikes.

✴ Take a wide variety of phys ed and health-club classes.

✴ Establish a personal yoga practice. Go to specialty yoga workshops.

✴ Practice your martial art daily. Improve your skills and earn higher belts.

✴ Read books and magazines about your fitness interests: bodybuilding, karate, yoga, Pilates, aerobics, etc.

✴ If your school offers them, take classes in human anatomy, muscle and skeletal groups, and exercise science.

✴ Volunteer to assist teachers in exercise, yoga, or martial arts classes.

# The Inside Scoop: Q&A

**Paula Lynch**
**Yoga instructor**
**New York, New York**

**Q:** *How did you get your job?*

**A:** Yoga Works offers one of the most comprehensive yoga training programs, so I started by committing to their 500-hour training, which I did over the course of two years.

**Q:** *What do you like best about your job?*

**A:** I love connecting with people on different levels and helping students understand themselves a little better through their yoga practice. I see the body as an amazing vehicle through which we can access the deeper layers of ourselves; teaching asana [poses] allows me to present students with the challenge of connecting their bodies with their breath and tapping into the subtle and energetic layers of the self. We can learn so much about ourselves simply by threading our movements with our breath and listening to how the body responds. I feel really fortunate to be able to help students find this connection and humbled by how much I continue to learn from the students and the practice.

**Q:** *What's the most challenging part of your job?*

**A:** I am both challenged and inspired by all the different people that come to yoga. The diversity of students presents challenges and lessons for me in teaching. It keeps me learning about the practice in new ways: how to apply the asana practice to specific students' needs and to invite students not to feel frustrated by what they may not be able to do yet, but what they can explore in their body and breath each time they practice.

**Q:** *What are the keys to success to being a yoga instructor?*

**A:** It is imperative that as a teacher you do your own practice with regularity, integrity and devotion. Good training is also very important, and to be continually learning on your own is essential.

# *What Training You'll Need*

You'll need your high school diploma. Certification in first aid and cardiopulmonary resuscitation (CPR) is a good idea. Then you may need to get a certification from a fitness organization to prove to prospective employers that you're qualified to teach some kind of exercise. Most health clubs won't give you on-the-job training, so you'd better know what you're doing when you start.

If you want to teach fitness classes at a gym or health club, you may be able to find work without getting certified. Health clubs mainly want to know that you can plan and lead a class. The best training includes taking lots of exercise classes yourself so that you know how a good class should be run. Getting certified is probably a good idea, though. Lots of health clubs require certification, and you'll be able to earn more money. To get certified, you have to pass a written test on human physiology and exercise techniques; there may be a practical test, too. Some certifying organizations offer training courses. There are many organizations offering certification; they include the Aerobics and Fitness Association of America (http://www.afaa.com) and the American Fitness Professionals Associates (http://www.afpafitness.com). Once you've got a job as a fitness instructor, you can take seminars and workshops to improve your knowledge.

If you want to be a personal trainer you'll also have to get certified. Several organizations offer training programs and certification exams. You should pick one that's accredited by the National Commission for Certifying Agencies (http://www.noca.org).

If you plan to teach yoga or martial arts you may not need certification. Martial arts disciplines often allow advanced students to start teaching. The yoga world has no formal certification requirements for teachers. If you're serious about teaching yoga, though, you ought to take a teacher training program. Many studios offer teacher training; look for one recognized by the Yoga Alliance (http://www.yoga alliance.org). Programs range from weekend workshops to year-long courses that require several hundred hours of work. Pilates instructors likewise do not necessarily need certification; However, the Pilates Method Alliance now offers certification as a way of ensuring quality control; they're a good place to look for teacher training programs. (http://www.pilatesmethodalliance.com).

# *How to Talk Like a Pro*

Here are a few words you'll hear as a fitness worker:

✴ **Body mass index (BMI)** This is a measurement of a person's weight in proportion to his or her height; the lower the BMI, the leaner the person is.

✴ **Certified personal trainer** A health and fitness professional who has received specific training and has passed an exam to show his or her competence to create exercise programs to help people achieve their fitness goals.

✴ **Human physiology** The study of how the human body works.

# *How to Find a Job*

Lots of fitness trainers find jobs through word of mouth. If you have friends who work in the fitness industry, ask them about job possibilities. If you exercise at a health club and would like to work there, go see the manager and ask for a job application. Volunteer to help teach at your yoga studio or martial arts studio—it could lead to a paying job. Look for advertisements in the local newspaper or online on job sites such as Monster.com (http://www.monster.com). Do an Internet search for "personal trainer" or "fitness instructor" plus your hometown. You never know who might be looking for someone. Universities often advertise for fitness workers. You can sometimes find job announcements on bulletin boards at colleges. The AFPA and other organizations have job boards on their Web sites.

If you want to work as a group instructor, you will interview with the manager of the gym or studio to which you are applying. However, if you're a personal trainer you might interview directly with your clients. When you go to an interview, dress in neat clothes; casual or exercise clothing is generally appropriate for interviews at gyms and studios, as long as it's not revealing or ratty. You may have to teach a sample class. If so, arrive on time, dressed to teach in clothing suited for your specialty. Tell the employer all about your experience and training in the fitness field, emphasizing your specialty. Show your enthusiasm and pleasant personality. Remember, the employer will want you to make customers want to keep coming to the gym and to bring all their friends, too!

# Secrets for Success

See the following suggestions and turn to the appendix for advice on résumés and interviews.

★ Smile! People want to work out with a trainer or instructor who makes them feel good. When you teach, try to make your classes or training sessions fun as well as strenuous.

★ Never single anyone out for negative comment—that's embarrassing, and clients hate it.

# Reality Check

Are you confident about your personal appearance? You'd better be. When you teach fitness classes, groups of strangers will watch your every move. As a personal trainer, you'll be very close to your clients when you assist them. Good personal grooming is a must!

# Some Other Jobs to Think About

★ Recreation worker. You'll organize recreational programs for communities, cities, churches, summer camps, theme parks, or tourist attractions. There's lots of summer and part-time work in this field.

★ Assistant coach. You'll help a sports coach run team practices and games. This is a great job for a high school athlete.

★ Referee/umpire. Sports leagues always need people who can referee games. Only try this if you don't mind fans yelling at you.

# How You Can Move Up

★ Become a fitness manager. To manage a gym or studio, you'll likely need an associate's degree in fitness management.

★ Become a physical therapy assistant. Physical therapy is growing as fast as fitness work, and physical therapy technicians can earn good money. You'll need to go to community college to get an associate's degree, but working as a personal trainer is a great way to get started.

✦ Get a college degree in exercise science or physical education. This will allow you to get a job teaching physical education in a school or college, which can be a more secure job than working part-time in health clubs.

## Web Sites to Surf

**American Council on Exercise** This organization certifies personal trainers and fitness instructors.   http://www.acefitness.org

**National Strength and Conditioning Association Certification Commission** This organization is just for strength-training specialists.   http://www.nscac.org

**Yoga Alliance.** This organization certifies yoga teachers and runs yoga training programs.   http://www.yogaalliance.org

Work with color and ink all day

# Tattoo and Piercing Specialist

Draw permanent illustrations on clients' skin

Pierce ears, noses, navels, and other body parts

# Tattoo and Piercing Specialist

Tattoo artists and piercers specialize in making permanent cosmetic changes to peoples' bodies. Tattoo artists do this by creating ink images on clients' arms, chests, or other body areas. They use hollow needles filled with ink to lightly pierce the skin with the help of a machine that moves the needle rapidly. Piercers put holes in their clients' bodies to allow them to wear body jewelry. Tattooing and piercing are ancient arts found in many cultures, including Tahitian (the Tahitian word *tatu* means "to mark"), Hindu, and many African traditions. Today tattoos and body piercings are increasingly popular fashion statements. Even so, these professions attract people who tend to be unconventional and adventurous. They also attract perfectionists—only people who like to be perfect can thrive in a field in which they permanently alter bodies.

## Is This Job for You?

To find out if a career as a tattoo artist or body piercer is right for you, read each of the following statements and answer "Yes" or "No."

Yes No **1.** Are you comfortable touching other peoples' bodies?

Yes No **2.** Are you imaginative and able to interpret people's artistic visions?

Yes No **3.** Are you comfortable with the thought of causing pain to someone else by cutting them or sticking them with needles?

Yes No **4.** Are you comfortable with the sight of blood?

Yes No **5.** Do you have a steady hand?

Yes No **6.** Are you good at drawing and painting?

Yes No **7.** Are you prepared to spend months or years as an apprentice before working on your own?

Yes No **8.** Are you willing to sterilize all your equipment every time you use it?

Yes No **9.** Would you like to be your own boss?

Yes No **10.** Are you unconventional and independent?

If you answered "Yes" to most of these questions, you may have the talent to pursue a career as a tattoo artist or piercer. To find out more about these jobs, read on.

## *Let's Talk Money*

Income in this field is highly variable. A yearly income of $20,000 a year is about average. However, location, local competition, and experience all affect earnings. Top artists command $100 per hour or more, which could give them a yearly income around $100,000.

# *What You'll Do*

As a tattoo artist, you'll draw and color permanent illustrations on the skin of your customers. When a customer arrives, you'll ask for proof of age (in most states it's illegal to tattoo people under the age of 18) and make sure the patron isn't drunk or on drugs. You'll give him or her a form to sign consenting to be tattooed and promising not to sue you if he or she is unhappy with the result, or if something goes wrong, such as the tattoo getting infected.

Some customers will select images from posters or catalogs in the shop, and others will bring their own pictures to you. They may ask you to adapt stock patterns to their desires, or to make custom designs just for them. You may sketch designs on paper before making them into tattoos. After you finalize the design, you'll use a machine to make a copy of the design, which you'll then transfer directly to the client's skin. This allows the client to see the design in place and gives you an outline to follow. You'll wash your hands, put on disposable gloves, and open a new, sterile needle and new, sterile containers of ink. You'll then use an electric tattoo machine to draw the outline and fill in the picture with colored inks. This aspect is similar to drawing or painting with pencils, except that it's on a person's body and it's permanent. You'll instruct the customer on caring for the new tattoo, such as by bandaging it or applying ointment to it.

As a piercing specialist, you'll make holes in clients' bodies that will allow them to wear metal jewelry. When a customer arrives, after discussing the piercing procedure, you'll have him or her sign a consent form. You'll wash your hands, put on disposable gloves, sterilize the piece of jewelry and wash the customer's skin. You'll then remove a new, sterile needle from its packaging and push it through the customer's skin in the correct location, perhaps using a piercing gun or other implement. You'll insert the jewelry, fasten it, and explain to the customer how to care for the piercing, such as by soaking it in salt water.

Safety is extremely important in these fields. Both tattoo artists and piercers always throw away their gloves and sterilize their equipment after working on a customer.

## *Who* You'll Work For

* ✴ A tattoo parlor or studio
* ✴ A piercing studio
* ✴ A mall's piercing shop
* ✴ Yourself

## *Where* You'll Work

As a tattoo artist, you'll work in a tattoo parlor, shop, or studio. Most tattoo parlors are fairly small. They can be in stand-alone buildings or in spaces in shopping centers or strip malls. You may spend some time working at the reception desk. The walls may be decorated with posters depicting various tattoo designs. The shop may offer various tattoo styles, such as black and gray (a style that originated in prisons); traditional American motifs such as hearts; highly detailed, fine line tattoos; full-body Asian styles; and popular tribal and Celtic motifs.

The studio itself may contain several small rooms where several artists can work, or it may contain one larger work area with curtains to partition different sections and protect the privacy of clients. In these areas, you'll keep your tattoo machines, inks, needles, gloves, razors, and autoclaves (sterilizing machines) used to sterilize your

## *Let's Talk Trends*

Body modifications are increasingly accepted in the United States. Experts estimate that about 15 percent of Americans have piercings in places other than their earlobes, or tattoos. Teens, soccer moms, and corporate professionals all sport body art these days, and many employers now allow visible tattoos and piercings at work.

equipment. You'll have some chairs for clients to sit on and a table for them to lie on so that they can be positioned properly for you to work on them.

If you become a piercer, you may work at a piercing studio, though it's more likely that you'll work along with tattoo artists at a tattoo studio. The piercing area will also have a table for clients to lie on and chairs for them to sit on, an autoclave, various piercing implements, and your collection of piercing jewelry to put in newly pierced holes.

## *Your* Typical Day

Here are the highlights of a typical day for tattooist and piercer.

- ✔ **Open at noon.** A young woman asks you to tattoo a flower on her lower back. You make an initial pencil sketch, and use a machine to make a copy that lets you transfer the design onto her skin. She doesn't like its placement so you wipe it off and reapply. Once she's satisfied, you proceed with the tattoo.
- ✔ **Design a fish tattoo.** A young man wants a large Asian fish on his ribs. You spend an hour sketching the design for his approval. Over the next hour, you tattoo the outline of the fish on his ribs in black ink. He'll have to come back later for you to fill in the colors.
- ✔ **Finish with a piercing.** Your last client of the day chooses a new belly-button ring from the shop's selection. You attach a surgical clamp to the top of her navel to stabilize the tissue, remove a sterile piercer from the autoclave, push it through her skin, and insert the ring. Before you leave for the night, you sterilize all your equipment and dispose of your needles in a proper container.

## *What* You Can Do Now

- ✳ Work on your art. Practice drawing and painting so that you'll have a portfolio to show a prospective teacher.
- ✳ Read tattoo magazines. Visit tattoo Web sites, such as tattoodles.com and learn about various tattoo styles.
- ✳ Save your money. An apprenticeship with a tattoo artist or piercer may cost thousands of dollars.

# The Inside Scoop: Q&A

**Adam Duncan**
**Tattooer**
**Asheville, North Carolina**

**Q:** *How did you get your job?*

**A:** I apprenticed between the ages of 16 and 18 under a tattoo artist who took me on, then worked in other shops for a few years. Ace of Spades is the nicest shop in Asheville and I wanted to work there. To get a job as a tattooer, you need a portfolio and you have to go meet people. If you just call they won't hire you. I had a portfolio of five or six years of my work, and they hired me on the spot.

**Q:** *What do you like best about your job?*

**A:** I like that I can do art all day and all night, all the time. I mean, even if I'm not tattooing, I'm drawing and painting. I like painting. It's a job where I can paint all day and make a living. It's not really a job; it's my life—I don't even think of it as a job.

**Q:** *What's the most challenging part of your job?*

**A:** You've got to do perfect work every day. You've got to leave your emotional stuff at home and be perfect.

**Q:** *What are the keys to success to being a tattoo artist?*

**A:** You have to live it. You have to always, always think of art. To be a tattooer, it's got to be your life. I don't know about everyone else, but I'm like that, and I'm a successful tattooer.

## What Training You'll Need

Most tattoo artists and piercers learn their craft through an apprenticeship. Other training methods such as seminars or schools are available, but professional piercing and tattoo organizations recommend apprenticeships as the best way of learning these trades. You'll have to learn how to apply designs to different types and colors of skin, which doesn't behave like paper. In addition to perfecting your drawing and painting skills, you'll study how to adapt existing designs and create new ones, how to do different types of piercing, how to protect a client's modesty, how to keep your equipment safe and sterile, and how to handle customers.

Not all tattoo artists or piercers want apprentices, and there is a lot of competition for spots with the best artists. This means that finding an apprenticeship can be hard. Look for an established practitioner with several years of experience and ask him or her to take you as a student. Try to find a studio that looks clean. The artist will want to see samples of your drawing, so bring a portfolio of your best artwork.

The bad news: You won't make money from your apprenticeship, so you'll need a source of income to support yourself and to pay your apprenticeship fees to your teacher. If the artist accepts you as an apprentice, you'll have to sign a contract agreeing to terms; expect to pay several thousand dollars for your training. You'll spend three years or so sweeping the floor, answering phones, and doing other boring jobs in addition to gradually learning how to make tattoos or piercings. A good teacher will let you observe procedures and then supervise you when you attempt them yourself. You'll learn about disease transmission, sterilization, disinfection, cross-contamination, and anatomy. Your teacher will decide when you've learned enough to be a competent tattoo artist or piercer. There are no diplomas or official certifications yet available to prove competence. Some states have licensing requirements, so you may have to take a test or prove that you've taken certain classes before you can practice on your own. If you think you may want to open your own studio one day, take a class in business and entrepreneurship at your local community college.

## *How to Talk Like a Pro*

Here are some terms you'll hear working as a tattoo and piercing specialist:

- ✴ **Autoclave** A machine that uses heat and steam to kill germs on things.
- ✴ **Body modification** Changing someone's body permanently, such as by piercing it or tattooing the skin.
- ✴ **Pigment** A substance that gives paint or dye its particular color.

* **Septum** The piece of skin at the bottom of the nose between the nostrils.
* **Sharps** Sharp items such as needles. You won't throw away disposable needles with normal garbage because they can hurt garbage workers. Instead, you dispose of them as medical waste in special containers.

# How to Find a Job

Most tattoo and piercing studios don't advertise their need for artists and piercers. Once you've completed your apprenticeship, you may be able to keep working at your teacher's studio, or you may decide to find a job somewhere else. The best way to get a job is to walk into a tattoo and piercing shop and show the owner your portfolio of work. Show that you know about current trends and traditional styles, such as Celtic designs or Chinese lettering. Local tattoo and piercing communities tend to be small, and most of the local professionals will know one another. Word-of-mouth recommendations can help you move from shop to shop. If you want to work in the top shops, practice your skills until they are perfect.

You can also network by going to or volunteering at tattoo and piercing gatherings and conventions, watching technique demonstrations, and talking to accomplished tattoo and piercing artists.

Safety and sterilization are also very important in the tattoo and piercing industry today, and your prospective employer will want to know that you will take safety seriously. Explain what training you've had in first aid and hygiene.

# Secrets for Success

See the following suggestions and turn to the appendix for advice on résumés and interviews.

* The best tattoos stay crisp and bright for a lifetime. All tattoos, particularly fine-line and photorealistic images, are prone to "smearing" as the inks move under the skin. The best artists know exactly how much ink to apply so that the image stays unmarred by spreading ink.
* Be attune to the psychology of your clients as you explore with them the possibility of adding creating permanent artwork on their body.

# *Reality Check*

Some of your prospective clients will come to get tattoos after drinking or taking drugs. Be careful about agreeing to tattoo anyone who isn't completely in their right mind; they may regret it later and blame you!

# *Some Other Jobs to Think About*

✴ Massage therapist. If you enjoy working with peoples' bodies, but don't like the idea of sticking needles into anyone, massages are a great way to make people relax, reduce stress, and feel better generally. If you like to work with needles therapeutically, consider training to become an acupuncturist.

✴ Makeup artist or manicurist. If you like to decorate other peoples' bodies, you can do it without breaking skin—using makeup or nail polish. You could even paint "tattoos" on people!

✴ Laser technician. Laser hair removal and skin rejuvenation are big these days. You may even find yourself removing tattoos.

# *How You Can Move Up*

✴ Learn specialty tattoo and piercing techniques. There are lots of different types of tattoos, including Japanese and photorealistic styles, and colorful feminine tattoos are popular with women. If you can create a variety of styles, you'll be in higher demand. Not every shop does all types of piercing; if you learn the more extreme types, you'll have rare and marketable skills.

✴ Own your own tattoo and piercing shop. The tattooists and piercers who make the most money are usually the ones who own their own businesses. You'd have to handle all the details of a business, from buying insurance and paying rent and taxes to hiring and firing employees.

# Web Sites to Surf

**Alliance of Professional Tattooists.** This organization was founded in 1992 to educate tattoo artists about the need for sterilization and other health precautions. The site includes membership information and a list of frequently asked questions for customers.   http://www.safe-tattoos.com

**Association of Professional Piercers.** This professional organization's site has information on how to become a piercer, membership information, a job board, and lots of articles about piercing.   http://www.safepiercing.org

Care for babies and toddlers

# Nanny, Babysitter, Day Care Assistant

Watch little ones grow and change daily

Get and give lots of hugs

# Nanny, Babysitter, Day Care Assistant

Do you like babies? Does the idea of spending your day surrounded by toddlers and little kids appeal to you? Child care is a growing field with plenty of opportunity. A growing number of parents need babysitters, nannies, or other child care professionals to watch their children when they work. Most of today's families have both parents in the workforce or are headed by a single working parent. According to the U.S. Department of Labor, 70.5 percent of all mothers worked full- or part-time in 2005, including 53.8 percent of mothers with children under age one. Babysitting or working in a day care center is a great way to see the world from a child's-eye view. It also offers a fascinating opportunity to watch babies grow through unique stages and learn to express themselves. Though turnover is high, many child care professionals wouldn't trade their positions for the world. Dedicated child care workers share one common trait: They really love children and enjoy caring for them.

## Is This Job for You?

To find out if being a child care worker is right for you, read each of the following questions and answer "Yes" or "No."

Yes   No   **1.** Do you do really like babies and toddlers?

Yes   No   **2.** Are you very patient and loving?

Yes   No   **3.** Are you creative?

Yes   No   **4.** Do you like taking care of children?

Yes   No   **5.** Are you outgoing and energetic?

Yes   No   **6.** Are you good at inventing and leading games?

Yes   No   **7.** Would you mind doing repetitive tasks, such as reading the same book repeatedly or changing diapers every couple of hours?

Yes   No   **8.** Do you enjoy watching babies and small children grow and develop?

Yes   No   **9.** Are you thorough about sanitation and cleanliness?

Yes   No   **10.** Can you stay calm when children are crying or throwing tantrums?

If you answered "Yes" to most of these questions, you may have the talent to pursue a career as a babysitter, nanny, or day care assistant. To find out more about these jobs, read on.

## *Let's Talk Money*

The average child care worker earns about $8.75 an hour, or a little more than $18,000 per year, according to 2006 data from the U.S. Bureau of Labor Statistics. The highest paid child care workers average over $26,000. A majority nannies and babysitters work part-time and do not receive benefits.

# *What You'll Do*

Child care workers, including nannies, babysitters, and day care workers, take care of small children when their parents can't. If you find a job as a nanny or babysitter, you'll care for the children of a single family in that family's home. You'll play with the kids, dress them, bathe them, change their diapers or help them use the toilet, read them books, and supervise their naps. Depending on your hours, you may even put them to bed at night. You'll make and serve them meals, from bottles to real food. Some parents will expect you to do some light housecleaning. You will also enforce your employer's rules. For instance, your children may not be allowed to watch television—some parents are very particular about this. If you care for school-age kids, you may pick them up after school and shuttle them around to activities and sports practices.

Day care workers handle larger groups of kids in age-segregated groups. If you work at a day care center, you will probably be assigned to one group of children, such as the older babies (crawlers and walkers who would run all over smaller infants) or the two-and-a-half-year-olds. The number of children will determine how many coworkers you have; states require specific ratios of child care workers to children, depending on the age of the kids. Experts recommend low ratios of children to caregivers because children do best if they have plenty of adult attention. The American Academy of Pediatrics, for instance, recommends that a caregiver work with no more than three infants under one year, or four children between the ages of 13 months and 30 months, or five children between 31 and 35 months. As a day care worker, you'll greet parents and children, feed babies or get snacks and lunches for older kids, and repeatedly teach simple lessons such as "We share," or "We help." You'll also change diapers or monitor toilet runs, run or help with playtime, leading songs and hand games, overseeing the dress-up and other play areas. You'll also settle children down for their naps.

## *Who* You'll Work For

* A day care center
* A family
* A corporation
* A church
* A community center
* An after-school program

## *Where* You'll Work

If you work for a family as a nanny, you'll probably spend a good portion of your workdays in that family's home. You'll take care of the family's babies or toddlers while the parents go out to work. You'll spend most of your time in the children's bedrooms or playrooms, but you may go around the rest of the house and yard. Some rooms may be off limits to you and the kids. You'll be around valuable items and you'll have to prove to the parents that you're trustworthy and won't steal their things. The parents may give you a house key and teach you the code for their security system so that you can come and go during the day. They may also lend you a car to use for taking children to appointments and playdates.

## *Let's Talk Trends*

Of the 1.3 million child care workers in the United States, one-third are self-employed. (Of those about two-thirds work for individual families as nannies or babysitters, and others worked as babysitters for multiple families.) The rest work for day care centers or they care for children in their own homes. A baby boomlet has lead to an increase in the need for child care workers, and this trend is expected to increase. What's more, high job turnover due to low pay means plenty of hiring opportunities.

The majority of child care workers are employed by various types of day care centers. These businesses usually have several rooms for children of different ages. Most day care centers group kids by age so toddlers aren't in the same room as infants. Infant rooms contain cribs so the babies can take their naps. Toddler rooms often have a closet full of cots or mats for naptime. All rooms will have age-appropriate toys. The center will probably have some small tables and tiny chairs for lunch and snacks. It will have changing tables for diapering babies and tiny toilets for potty "trainees." Most day care centers have an outdoor playground with miniature playground equipment. You'll spend lots of your time outside supervising playing children.

# *Your* Typical Day

Here are the highlights of a typical day for a day care assistant in the infant room.

✔ **Greet parents and babies.** Between 7:30 a.m. and 8:30 a.m., as parents drop off their babies, you and your coworker in the infant room offer the children and their parents a warm welcome. You hear who has sniffles, who's teething, and you listen to the special instructions a few parents pass along. You also help them place their babies in their assigned cribs or bouncy seats. You also place bottles of formula and breast milk labeled with each baby's name in the refrigerator.

✔ **Help with feeding time.** At 10:00 a.m. you put bottles in a bottle warmer; when they're tepid, you and your colleague start feeding the six babies in the room. Three can hold their own bottles. You feed two of them baby food from jars. After eating, everyone gets a fresh diaper.

✔ **Facilitate rest and play.** Most of the babies sleep for the next two hours; you rock one who is having trouble falling asleep. After nap time you put mats on the floor for baby playtime. You roll a ball back-and-forth to one baby who can sit up, and hold another on your lap while you read a picture book. You put the three oldest in a wagon and take them for a ride around the block while your colleague sings to the other three, who are playing with infant gyms. Just before pickup time, you give the afternoon bottles and change diapers again.

# The Inside Scoop: Q&A

**Raquel Melesio**
**Day care assistant**
**Austin, Texas**

**Q:** *How did you get your job?*

**A:** I was hired to fill in for my sister's position for the summer. I was going to leave when she returned. But I loved my job and the people who run Children's Discovery Center loved me, and they asked me to stay as a full-time teacher.

**Q:** *What do you like best about your job?*

**A:** I love the big smiles and hugs from each of my lovebugs every day.

**Q:** *What's the most challenging part of your job?*

**A:** Not letting myself get frustrated over simple, little basic things, such as when I try to accomplish too many tasks at one time. It's also hard when my babies move up to the next classroom!

**Q:** *What are the keys to success to being a day care assistant?*

**A:** Have patience! I have to remember that these are still small children who are learning about this big environment they are in each day. Remember it's okay to "take five" to stay alive. If you don't you will get burned out quickly. Your heart and mind have got to be a big part of why you are there.

## What You Can Do Now

- ✸ Babysit.
- ✸ Volunteer in your church or community center nursery.
- ✸ Take courses on cardiopulmonary resuscitation (CPR) and child care.
- ✸ Take courses in child development, if your high school offers them.

✦ Visit your high school career counselor to get information on careers in child care.

✦ Read books, magazines, and Web sites about babies and children.

# *What* Training *You'll Need*

Though your job may not require you to have training, any training you can get will put you ahead of the competition and make you a more knowledgeable, professional child care worker. Many babysitters and nannies learn how to take care of children by helping at home with their own brothers and sisters or other children of relatives. Others gain experience babysitting in middle school and high school or helping out at their church nurseries. Try to take at least some courses on child development. There are a lot of myths about babies. For instance, did you know that babies can't be spoiled? A good child development course will clear up many of these myths. Similarly, it's also important to know the latest safety information about babies. Did you know that it's dangerous to put an infant to sleep on his or her stomach? Courses can also teach you how to keep babies and toddlers happy and safe at each stage of development. No amount of training, however, can take the place of patience and kindness.

Some states have licensing requirements for child care workers in day care centers. You may need to prove that you've graduated from high school; some states will require you to take specialized courses at a community college. Some employers will want you to earn a credential such as child development associate (CDA) or certified child care professional (CCP). To get a CDA credential, you'll need to have a high school diploma or equivalent, have 480 hours of experience working with children in the past five years, and take 120 hours of formal child care course. The CCP credential requires more, 720 hours work and 180 hours of education; you'll also have to create a portfolio that shows what you can do, be observed by a more experienced teacher, take an exam, and pay a fee of $495.

If you drive children to their school or lessons, you'll also need a driver's license. Most employers will want you to get certified in first aid and CPR. In these courses, offered by your local Red Cross, you'll learn how to bandage small injuries and how to tell when a child should see a doctor. You'll also learn emergency techniques such as how to resuscitate a child who has stopped breathing or how to help a child who is choking. There are many child care skills that you'll either learn from your employer or through experience, such as proper diapering procedures. Most day care centers will require you to wear disposable gloves and sterilize the changing table between changes to avoid spreading diseases. You'll learn how to heat bottles for small infants and how to feed older babies and children. You'll have to learn how to entertain your charges, which can be quite a challenge! It can take several weeks or months to get completely comfortable with caring for babies and toddlers.

# *How to Talk Like a Pro*

Here are some terms you hear working in the field of child care:

- ✸ **Cardiopulmonary resuscitation (CPR)** A first aid technique used on a person who has stopped breathing and whose heart may have stopped beating. Techniques for infants and children differ from CPR techniques for adults.
- ✸ **Caregiver** A person who takes care of a child or children.
- ✸ **Early childhood development** The way babies and toddlers grow and develop in their first years. All children acquire certain skills, generally within a given time frame. For example, most babies start walking between 10 and 16 months, with a few stragglers waiting until 18 months to toddle.

# *How to Find a Job*

Many nannies and babysitters find jobs through word of mouth. Tell your friends and acquaintances that you want to work as a babysitter, and chances are a family will call you out of the blue asking you to work for them. You can also make a flier and post it at schools or workplaces with bulletin boards, or run advertisements in community or group newsletters. As you gain experience and references, you should be able to find one or two families that can offer you full-time employment or substantial part-time work. Some nannies and babysitters work through agencies, however. A nanny service may want you to hold some certifications or at least have a high school diploma.

If you want to work at a day care center, look for ads in your local newspaper's classified section. You can also visit day care centers in person to introduce yourself to the owners or managers. Turnover is high in the industry so chances are good that you'll find an opening. If you don't, consider volunteering a few hours a week in a day care center, so that the day care director can observe your work and attitude firsthand.

However you go about finding a job, show your prospective employer that you're reliable, punctual, and friendly. Show up on time for an interview. Show your genuine interest in the children and the job. You'll need to provide references and perhaps undergo a criminal check. Before you look for a job, ask previous employers or teachers if they would be willing to answer questions about you and your work habits.

## *Secrets for Success*

See the following suggestions and turn to the appendix for advice on résumés and interviews.

* Share anecdotes with parents. Moms and dads love to hear about what their child did each day. Make a mental note (or write down) an observation each for each child you care for, such as something funny she said or a new achievement he is working on. The parents you work for will be grateful.
* As your charges age out of your care, new clients will fill in if you have a good rapport with other parents in the community.

## *Reality Check*

No one goes into child care work expecting to get rich, and you shouldn't either. The pay is low and most workers don't get benefits such as health insurance. The hours can be really long, too, and some centers are too busy for the workers to take breaks.

## *Some Other Jobs to Think About*

* Preschool aide. If you like working with kids but think you might prefer older kids, consider assisting the teacher at a preschool, kindergarten, or elementary school.
* Nurse's aide. You'll work in a hospital or clinic, helping nurses take care of patients. If you work for a pediatric clinic, you'll assist babies and little kids.

# *How You Can Move Up*

✴ Be an entrepreneur. Open your own day care center or nanny/babysitting service, or become a manager/administrator of a day care center. You'll select employees who will take care of other people's children, either at your own day care center or in clients' homes. You'll need a good head for business and excellent customer service skills. You'll need to be state-certified as well.

✴ Become a teacher's assistant. You'll still get to work with kids, but you won't have to do the heavy lifting required of a classroom teacher.

✴ Become a teacher. There are lots of opportunities for teachers at all levels, from preschool up to high school. You'll have to get a bachelor's degree, but you'll be around kids and make a real difference in their lives. You'll also get summer vacation time.

✴ Become a social worker or social work assistant. Social workers need at least a bachelor's degree, and more typically, a master's. However, social work assistant positions are easier to get and require only an associate's degree. Depending on your job placement, you may have a great deal of contact with children, and lots of opportunities to help people.

## **Web Sites to Surf**

**International Nanny Association.** This is a good spot for would-be nannies to look for information.  http://www.nanny.org

**National Association for the Education of Young Children.** If you're interested in early childhood education, this is a good resource.  http://www.naeyc.org

**National Child Care Association.** This group offers licenses to child care providers.  http://www.nccanet.org

**National Child Care Information Center.** The U.S. Department of Health and Human Services runs this site to provide information on child care to parents, workers, researchers, and the public.  http://www.nccic.org

**Zero to Three.** This Web site provides information on various topics of baby and child development.  http://www.zerotothree.org

Be part of a teaching team

# Preschool Aide, School Aide

Spend your days working with kids

Make a real difference in a child's life

# *Preschool Aide, School Aide*

Preschool aides and school aides—also called "paras" (for paraprofessional), teacher aides, or "assistants"—spend their days helping classroom teachers with their daily work. In 2005, there were nearly 1.3 million school aides working in the United States. Recent federal laws require some schools to hire additional teaching aides, so the job outlook for aides is positive. It's especially good for anyone with two years of college, who speaks a foreign language, who has training in caring for students with disabilities, or who is willing to work in schools with high poverty levels. Working as a preschool or school aide is a wonderful job for anyone who enjoys children and wants to be part of an educational team.

To find out if being a preschool or school aide is right for you, read each of the following questions and answer "Yes" or "No."

| | | | |
|---|---|---|---|
| *Yes* | *No* | **1.** | Do you enjoy working with children? |
| *Yes* | *No* | **2.** | Are you patient? |
| *Yes* | *No* | **3.** | Are you organized and reliable? |
| *Yes* | *No* | **4.** | Are you neat and do you know how to keep a room clean? |
| *Yes* | *No* | **5.** | Are you good at classroom activities and projects? |
| *Yes* | *No* | **6.** | Can follow directions well? |
| *Yes* | *No* | **7.** | Can you communicate clearly with both children and parents? |
| *Yes* | *No* | **8.** | Do you like to organize games and activities for groups of children? |
| *Yes* | *No* | **9.** | Are you good at solving problems? |
| *Yes* | *No* | **10.** | Are you comfortable using a computer? |

If you answered "Yes" to most of these questions, you may have the talent to pursue a career as a teacher aide. To find out more about this job, read on.

## *Let's Talk Money*

Many preschool and school aides work part-time for an hourly wage. Preschool aides make about $8.50 an hour (about $10,000 per school year), depending on region and experience. The average salary for teacher aides is about $21,200 (Bureau of Labor Statistics, 2005 data).

# *What You'll Do*

If you work as a teacher or preschool aide, you could find yourself doing almost any job you can think of. Teacher aides and preschool aides help classroom teachers, performing various necessary jobs so that teachers have more time to teach and plan lessons. In many cases, aides do nearly the same jobs as teachers. Some aides help with lessons and classroom work. Others do mostly nonacademic work, such as monitoring playgrounds and cafeterias.

If you become a school aide, you may spend much of your time helping students with their lessons. You may read stories, help children read, write, or work out their math problems, or your may supervise art projects. The teacher may put you in charge of keeping the classroom stocked with supplies. You may take attendance, collect homework, and grade papers. If you're good with computers, you may be put in charge of the class computer lab.

The younger the children at the school, the more attention they will need. If you work at a preschool, you'll have to help the children get dressed to go outside and watch them closely while they play. You'll probably tie dozens of shoes every day, and you may have to dry occasional tears. You even may have to mop up "accidents." If you work at an elementary school or a middle school, the students will look up to you as a role model. You may have to enforce discipline, perhaps inspecting bathrooms or breaking up playground fights. Special-needs students may demand lots of your time; you may work one-on-one with a special-needs student who requires help with every activity, including feeding, dressing, and boarding the school bus.

# *Who You'll Work For*

* Public schools, kindergarten through 12th grade
* Private schools, kindergarten through 12th grade
* After-school programs
* Summer programs
* Special teaching centers
* Public or private preschools
* Child care centers
* Religious organizations

## Let's Talk Trends

There are always jobs available for teacher aides and preschool aides. However, the biggest demand over the next few years will be for special education aides and aides who speak a foreign language. The populations of the South and West are growing rapidly, so these will be good areas in which to find jobs.

# *Where* **You'll Work**

School aides work in—you guessed it—schools. Preschool aides work in preschools, which are often much smaller than elementary schools. Preschools usually have brightly colored decorations on the walls and classroom toy collections in addition to preschool "work" materials, a small playground, and child-sized furniture. School aides work in public elementary, middle, or high schools, or in special education centers. If you work in a school, you may stay in a single classroom, or you may move from class to class or to the computer lab or library as you are needed. You may drive students in a school van. If you work with special-needs students, you may be assigned to a single student who requires assistance all day long. During the summer, you may have some flexibility. Many preschools stay open all year, so you may continue working during the summer. However the summer routine may include more outdoor activities and wading pools or sprinklers— wear sunscreen! If you work at a public or private school, you may be able to find jobs in a summer program, or you may use the summer to take classes and improve your educational credentials.

# *Your* **Typical Day**

Here are the highlights of a typical day for a preschool aide.

- ✔ **Start the day early.** You'll get to school around 7:30 a.m. to make sure everything is in place before the children arrive. When they do you'll greet them and their parents, help them hang up their coats, and get them settled in an activity center for free play before "circle time" starts.
- ✔ **Help with lessons.** You'll assist children with developmental activities such as learning their colors, using blocks to create

patterns and buildings, and predicting what's going to happen next as you reading a story aloud. During recess, you'll supervise playground fun. At lunch, you'll help the children get their lunches and drinks.

✓ **Help with naps and play.** After supervising nap time, you'll give the children a snack and then take them outside to play until their parents arrive. One child's parent is late, and you reassure her: "Mommy will be here soon." Once everyone's gone, you'll reorganize the classroom and help set up for the next day.

# *What You Can Do Now*

✗ Work with children. Babysit, volunteer with your church or community child care centers, help coach sports teams, or get a job at a summer camp.

✗ Get certified in first aid and cardiopulmonary resuscitation (CPR).

✗ Take classes in child development or early childhood education.

✗ Work on your reading, writing, math, and computer skills.

✗ Learn what your state requirements are to become a school aide.

# *What Training You'll Need*

Most preschools will hire aides who have a high school diploma. Some of them will want you to have several months' experience working either with children or in some other job that shows that you're a responsible employee. You'll probably need a valid driver's license and a current first aid and CPR certification. You'll need to be healthy and strong; preschool aides spend a lot of time sitting on the floor, lifting children, mopping and vacuuming, and running around the playground.

School aides in K–12 schools usually need more training than preschool aides. Different states and school districts have different requirements, but many of them will want you to have at least some college training and several months' experience working in child care. If you actually help teach children, you will need more college than if you just supervise playtime and lunch. If you work with special-needs children, you'll have to take classes in caring for the disabled. If you want to work at a Title I school—a school with a large number of students from low-income households—you will have to have a

# The Inside Scoop: Q&A

Kellie Mullinax
Preschool aide
Greenville, South Carolina

**Q:** *How did you get your job?*

**A:** My friend was working at a Montessori preschool that had a job opening. She asked me if I'd be interested, and I'd never worked with kids before. But I came in and interviewed and got the job.

**Q:** *What do you like best about your job?*

**A:** I enjoy the one-on-one work, like teaching sandpaper letters to the kids individually. In the Montessori method, the children can choose to have a lesson, and they can keep doing it or choose to do something else. I also like playing with the kids and observing them. They're very interesting, the way they are with their friends and other people.

**Q:** *What's the most challenging part of your job?*

**A:** Patience! It comes and it goes, I guess, but you always have to be patient. Explaining things is hard, too. Sometimes you have to tell a child not to do something and then explain why they can't, and it can be hard to make them understand.

**Q:** *What are the keys to success to being a preschool aide?*

**A:** It's important to enjoy kids, to like playing with them. You have to make the kids comfortable in their environment, so they'll have more of an open mind and be interested in what can teach them or whatever they choose to learn.

two-year degree or higher, to have attended at least two years of college, or to pass a local test proving that you can do the job. Some states require school aides to take a 30- or 40-hour training course to become certified. In many states you'll have to pass a test such as ParaPro (a test of your reading, writing, and math skills) to comply with the requirements of the federal law No Child Left Behind.

Once you start working as a school or preschool aide, you'll receive lots of on-the-job training, for instance, in organizing class materials, teaching methods, keeping records, running a school, and operating computers and audiovisual equipment. Your school district might also give you time away from work to take classes in education and may even pay your tuition in exchange for your continuing to teach for a certain length of time. Warning: Almost all preschools and schools will run a criminal background check on you before giving you a job. Stay out of trouble!

## *How to Talk Like a Pro*

Here are some terms you hear working as a preschool aide or school aide:

✦ **Education paraprofessional** A paraprofessional is a person who provides support and assistance to a professional. School aides of various types, including teacher aides, special education assistants, bilingual assistants, and preschool aides, are often called education paraprofessionals.

✦ **No Child Left Behind Act (NCLB)** This is a federal law passed in 2002 that sets standards for school performance. It requires all school aides who work in the classroom to be "highly qualified."

✦ **Montessori** This is an educational method used in many preschools. Montessori schools encourage children to work independently and to practice life skills such as washing dishes. It avoids tests, grades, and competition.

## *How to Find a Job*

Start by looking for advertisements searching for preschool or school aides. An Internet search for "preschool aide," "school aide," or "teacher assistant" plus your hometown may turn up several job openings. You can also simply contact the local schools that interest you. Send them a letter introducing yourself and expressing your interest in working as an aide. Include a high school transcript and any college transcripts you have, a résumé that lists your work experience (including any volunteer work you've done with children) and two or three people the school can contact for recommendations. If you've prepared lesson plans, you can include them in the package as well. When you go to a school for an interview, dress nicely and arrive on time. Convince the prospective employer that you're reliable, enthusiastic, and pleasant to work with.

If you're not sure a job as a school aide is right for you, you can try working as a substitute aide. This way you can see what it would be like to work with different ages and abilities of students, including special needs students.

# *Secrets for Success*

See the following suggestions and turn to the appendix for advice on résumés and interviews.

* Don't take conflicts personally. Preschool aides often field complaints from parents about problems the children have at school. Just listen and nod; don't try to argue or convince the parents that they're wrong.
* Get help when you need it. Lead teachers and other staff often will have experience of some job issue you're facing or of something similar to a situation that is challenging you with one or more of the children. Draw from their experience. One day you may be the one with advice to share.

# *Reality Check*

Teacher aides and preschool aides work hard for low pay. Don't expect to make lots of money. You may not get benefits such as health insurance, either; about 40 percent of school aides work part-time for an hourly wage without benefits.

# *Some Other Jobs to Think About*

* Library or media assistant. You'll work in the library or media center helping students find research materials and use computers and bringing audiovisual materials to classrooms for teachers.
* School secretary. You'll work in the school office, greeting visitors, and helping out behind the scenes.
* Playground or cafeteria assistant. If you can't or don't want to take the classes to get certified for classroom work, you can find a job watching students at recess, at lunch, or after school.

# *How You Can Move Up*

✦ Become a preschool or school teacher. Many preschool and school aides go to college part-time, taking classes in early childhood or elementary education. You can become a preschool teacher with a two-year associate's degree. A four-year education degree will make you eligible for teacher certification.

✦ Specialize. Some schools use specialized educational methods, such as the Montessori method. Special-needs teachers who can take care of children with disabilities are in high demand. Many schools need teachers and aides who can speak foreign languages. Any kind of specialty training will increase your job opportunities and earning potential.

## Web Sites to Surf

**American Federation of Teachers.** This is the federal teachers' union Web site. It has pages for paraprofessionals such as aides, including a list of certification requirements by state.   http://www.aft.org

**National Education Association.** This national organization provides information for teachers, aides, parents, and others interested in education. http://www.nea.org

Make your clients' homes or offices look great

# Housekeeper, Janitor, Maid, Cleaner

See immediate results of your effort

Start work with minimal training

# Housekeeper, Janitor, Maid, Cleaner

The cleaning field is one of the largest occupational fields in the United States. More than 4 million people work as maids, housekeepers, or janitors. There are tons of jobs available in a huge range of workplaces. After all, every business, school, hospital, and hotel needs a cleaning staff, and millions of homeowners pay for housecleaning. The entry requirements are low; you can start work the day after you finish high school, or earlier. The money's not bad and the job provides immediate gratification; you can see the difference your effort makes right away. If you don't mind hard physical work and want to get started earning money right away, this might be the field for you.

## Is This Job for You?

To find out if being a janitor or maid is right for you, read the following questions, and answer "Yes" or "No."

Yes No **1.** Do you like to clean things?
Yes No **2.** Do you enjoy housework and cleaning duties?
Yes No **3.** Are you strong and healthy?
Yes No **4.** Can you work on your feet for many hours at a time?
Yes No **5.** Can you sustain hard physical effort?
Yes No **6.** Can you follow directions well?
Yes No **7.** Can you work well either alone or on a team?
Yes No **8.** Do you like to work evenings or part-time?
Yes No **9.** Are you honest and trustworthy?
Yes No **10.** Are you punctual?

If you answered "Yes" to most of these questions, you may have the talent to pursue a career as a janitor or maid. To find out more about these jobs, read on.

## Let's Talk Money

Janitors average $21,120 a year, or $10.15 per hour; housekeepers and maids earn an average of $18,180 a year, or $8.74 per hour; and housekeeping managers earn over $32,000 a year, or $15.66 an hour, according to 2006 figures from the U.S. Bureau of Labor Statistics.

# *What You'll Do*

Janitors, maids, housekeepers, and other cleaning professionals perform a range of necessary tasks to keep the world's businesses, schools, and homes clean, sanitary, and running smoothly. Maids and housekeepers sweep, mop, dust, vacuum, and polish. If you work at a hotel, you'll remove and replace sheets and towels, scrub bathtubs and bathroom floors, clean toilets, and stock rooms with soap, shampoo, and lotion. In a luxury hotel, you'll turn down sheets and leave mints on pillows, and restock the minibar. If you work at a hospital, you'll have to help keep the work environment sterile by disinfecting bed frames and mattresses and washing everything with germ-killing cleaner. If you work in an office building, you'll probably have a rolling cart for your cleaning supplies. Your tasks may include cleaning toilets, stocking toilet paper and paper towels, mopping or vacuuming floors, washing windows, emptying trash, and dusting shelves. If you work in houses and apartments, your jobs may include washing dishes, clothes, and bedding, putting away laundry, making the beds, cleaning ovens, polishing silver, and running errands such as taking clothes to the dry cleaner. As a janitor, your work will include some heavier cleaning. You may shampoo rugs, wash walls, and move furniture. You may have to do minor repairs to faucets, lights, or air conditioners. You may have to spray for insects or trap rats.

Regardless of where you work, or whether you work as a maid or janitor, you'll be exposed to harsh chemicals. However, this is changing as some cleaning services specialize in eco-friendly cleaning techniques. They perform the usual cleaning services but use only biodegradable cleaning products. Such services are becoming more common as consumers grow more concerned about the environment.

If you become the supervisor of a team of housekeepers, you'll tell the workers what jobs they need to do and inspect their work when they're finished. You may have to fill out paperwork or electronic forms to report on your team's daily work.

# *Who You'll Work For*

★ Schools—from elementary schools to universities
★ Local or state governments
★ Stores and shopping malls

## Let's Talk Trends

There are always openings for janitors and housekeepers. There should be steady growth, especially in residential cleaning, as a growing number of families and working parents face a shortage of time for tasks such as cleaning, and also as an aging population loses the interest in and capacity for cleaning.

* Hospitals
* Hotels
* Corporations with office buildings
* Entertainment businesses, such as theaters
* Individual homeowners

## *Where You'll Work*

Cleaning professionals can work nearly anywhere. You may work in clients' houses, doing cleaning for specific families. If you want to clean houses, you can either work for yourself and have your clients pay you directly, or you can work for a maid service (often as part of a team). When you go into people's homes, you'll have to be extra careful not to break anything; most people feel nervous about letting strangers into their homes, and they may look to you first if something in the house gets broken or goes missing.

Lots of cleaners work in office buildings. You'll clean the hallways, bathrooms, conference rooms, and individual offices. Most office cleaning happens at night, when companies are closed. You could also work in a school, cleaning hallways, lunchrooms, offices, and classrooms. Most school janitors work during the day, though classrooms can only be cleaned when school is not in session. If you work in a hospital, you'll clean hallways, lobbies, offices, patients' rooms, and even operating rooms. Hotel maids clean public spaces such as lobbies, restaurants and gift shops, and individual hotel rooms and bathrooms. Some of your work may take place outside, in gardens and on walkways.

# The Inside Scoop: Q&A

**Yannira Gutierrez**
**Maid**
**Van Nuys, California**

**Q:** *How did you get your job?*

**A:** I got my job through the newspaper. I took the job as a temporary thing, but once I got into it I realized that it was good money and that it was something I enjoyed doing, so I made it my career and I've been doing it ever since.

**Q:** *What do you like best about your job?*

**A:** What I like best is the feeling of satisfaction from doing a good job. I get a very good feeling when I see a big smile from a client after a job well done. I like to have a client's approval of my work. I also like that when I do a good job I receive wonderful gifts of appreciation for my work. Another thing I like is my celebrity clientele; I get to meet famous people I would probably not get to meet at any other job.

**Q:** *What's the most challenging part of your job?*

**A:** Most challenging is the feeling I get when I have to go to a new house and I don't know the client, how the house is, or how the client will receive me. Another challenge is not knowing how dirty a house is until you see it. A client might tell you one thing over the phone, but when you arrive it's completely different. I just have to do the best job I can.

**Q:** *What are the keys to success to being a maid?*

**A:** I think the keys to success to being a maid are: Love what you do, have a good personality when it comes to dealing with people, take pride in what you do, and do good work so you can get referrals for more work.

# *Your Typical Day*

Here are the highlights of a typical day for a maid who works for a cleaning service.

✓ **Start at the office.** You arrive at your service's office at 8 a.m. to get your assignment for the day. You load your cleaning supplies into a van, and you and two coworkers drive to your first house.

✓ **Clean from top to bottom.** You have three hours to clean your first house. You and your partners divide the jobs; you take the kitchen, the living room, and the downstairs bathroom. You load the dishwasher, scrub down the counters, sweep, mop, clean the windows, the faucet and other metalwork, and move on to the next room.

✓ **Go to house number two.** You stop for a brief fast-food lunch, and then you drive to your next house. After you finish there, you drive back to your office, unload the van, and turn in your paperwork from the two houses.

# *What You Can Do Now*

✴ Practice cleaning your own house: Sweep, mop, make beds, and wash windows. Set times and see if you can get everything done in a few hours.

✴ Look online and in books to find out proper cleaning techniques from making a bed to removing stains or cleaning a shower curtain (visit http://www.marthastewart.com for some expert tips).

✴ Volunteer to help out a neighbor who may be elderly or otherwise have trouble cleaning his or her own house. This way you can start building up referrals.

✴ Begin collecting cleaning supplies and learn about the effectiveness of various ones.

✴ Get a part-time job—any job—so you can show prospective employers that you're already a reliable employee.

✴ Take shop classes so you'll know some basic repair techniques.

✴ Study basic math—cleaners sometimes need to work with numbers to measure cleaning supplies or run machines.

# *What Training You'll Need*

Most janitors, maids, and housekeepers don't have any formal training. You won't even need to finish high school, though it will improve your chances of advancement. If you've learned how to clean a house, make beds, wash windows, do dishes, and fold laundry at home then you already have many of the skills you'll need to clean houses.

If you go to work for a cleaning service or janitorial company, you'll learn most of your skills on the job. You'll work with an experienced janitor or housekeeper at first and he or she will teach you the essentials of the job. You'll start with the easiest jobs and gradually move up to more complicated tasks. Many housekeeping companies have training programs to teach you the specific skills you'll need. You'll learn how to sweep and mop, run a vacuum cleaner; and how to wax, buff, and polish floors. You'll learn about different kinds of cleaners and how to use them safely. You'll learn where to keep your cleaning equipment and supplies and how to stock your rolling cart. Your supervisor will teach you how to collect and dispose of garbage. Some of your training will involve safety and health regulations. A lot of the work that cleaners do could be dangerous if done incorrectly. You'll learn what to do if an accident occurs on the job.

If you work at a hotel, your colleagues or supervisors will teach you how to strip sheets off beds and replace them with new ones, how to hang up towels, and how to clean rooms and bathrooms. You'll have to learn how to tell when you can enter a room and how to speak to guests if you encounter them. After you've worked for a while as a janitor or cleaner, you may learn some basic repair skills. Lots of janitors get training in electricity and plumbing so that they can make simple repairs. If you become a supervisor, you'll attend occasional classes on new cleaning techniques and employee management.

# *How to Talk Like a Pro*

Here are some terms you may hear in the cleaning services field:

- **Grout** The solid gray or white substance between tiles on a floor or wall.
- **Linoleum** A type of flooring made of solid linseed oil and canvas or burlap backing; today vinyl flooring is often incorrectly referred to as linoleum.

⚡ **Laminate flooring** A flooring material made of synthetic materials that looks like natural flooring materials such as wood or marble; Pergo is a leading brand.

⚡ **Mildew** A fungus that grows on warm, damp surfaces such as shower curtains.

## How to Find a Job

Businesses are always looking for cleaners. You can find a job easily by reading your local newspaper's classified section or doing an Internet search for "maid" or "janitor" plus your hometown. You can also go in person to a business where you'd like to work and offer your services. Try maid services, large office buildings, schools, hospitals, or hotels. Another way to find jobs is to contact labor unions or state and local employment service offices.

If you want to clean houses on your own, you can place an online ad in a local town or city message board or in the newspaper classified section, or post fliers at churches or schools, advertising your services as a maid. Word of mouth is a great way to find jobs. If you do a good job ask him or her to spread the word. You can print business cards and give them out as well.

When you speak to a prospective employer, be polite, dress neatly, and arrive on time. If you've had other jobs, bring a list of them and include telephone numbers of past employers or clients so that your new boss can call them and ask about you.

## Secrets for Success

See the following suggestions and turn to the appendix for advice on résumés and interviews.

⚡ Attention to detail and directions is key. You may have to remember a long list of cleaning duties. If you do all your tasks well (it's easy to tell if something really is clean or not), you can hope for more and better work.

⚡ Learn to estimate the time it takes to do specific tasks. Once you know this, you can plan with clients and work partners, and you will be able to work with a little less stress because you will know you are running on time.

# *Reality Check*

Cleaning can be dangerous. Back pain and injuries from slipping and falling are common. To avoid injuries, lift heavy objects with your legs, not your back. Use extra care when walking on wet floors, and be aware of power cords and other objects on the floor so you don't trip over them.

# *Some Other Jobs to Think About*

⚹ Food preparation and service worker. As a restaurant worker, you'll perform lots of the same jobs that housekeepers and janitors do, cleaning and organizing your workplace. You'll also cook food and prepare it to be served.

⚹ Grounds maintenance worker. You'll work outdoors, mowing lawns, tending gardens, and maintaining outdoor landscape features.

⚹ Pest control worker. You'll study the habits of various pests, including roaches, ants, fleas, termites, bees, rats, and mice and learn how to eradicate them with traps and poisons.

⚹ Crime scene (forensics) cleaner. If you have a tough stomach, can follow directions well, and can learn to preserve evidence, you can earn high pay as a forensics cleaner.

# *How You Can Move Up*

⚹ Become a supervisor or manager of a cleaning team. This will be easiest if you work for a company that has lots of cleaners. You'll definitely need to finish high school or get your general educational development credential (GED) if you want to become a supervisor. A second language, such as Spanish, is particularly useful for managers.

⚹ Become an owner of a cleaning service. You'll hire housekeepers and janitors and send them out to clients. You'll need a good head for business and good people skills.

⚹ Become an executive housekeeper. This position, an actual certification provided to qualifying cleaning supervisors and managers by the International Executive Housekeepers Association, will allow you to manage teams of cleaners at large businesses such as hospitals or hotels. To become a certified executive housekeeper, you'll have to get an associate's degree in housekeeping from a college, take a 330-hour certification course, or complete a self-study program. Visit http://www.ieha.org for more information.

## Web Sites to Surf

**International Executive Housekeepers Association** This association provides benefits such as educational opportunities, conferences, resource materials, and certifications such as "registered executive housekeeper." http://www.ieha.org

**Merry Maids** This is one of the biggest maid service companies in the United States. Though the site is primarily directed at potential customers, it includes cleaning tips that could come in handy. http://www.merrymaids.com

Comfort the bereaved

# Funeral Attendant

Prepare the dead for burial

Be part of a funeral team

# Funeral Attendant

People die every day. It's not a pleasant thought, but it's true, and it's also true that every person who dies must be cared for in some way. That's where funeral attendants come in. Funeral attendants work for mortuaries or funeral homes doing essential jobs, some of which involve dead bodies and some of which include more ordinary tasks such as cleaning, arranging flowers, or setting up chairs. Though the jobs of most funeral attendants aren't quite as exciting as the ones portrayed on the hit cable show *Six Feet Under*, employees who work in this field find it deeply satisfying. They know they're doing a necessary job and helping the bereaved handle some of the most difficult moments of their lives.

## Is This Job for You?

To find out if being a funeral attendant is right for you, read the following questions, and answer "Yes" or "No."

Yes   No   **1.** Could you be comfortable working around dead bodies?

Yes   No   **2.** Are you comfortable being around people who are crying?

Yes   No   **3.** Are you polite and dignified, and do you dress neatly?

Yes   No   **4.** Are you strong enough to move furniture around?

Yes   No   **5.** Do you enjoy displaying flowers and candles?

Yes   No   **6.** Are you neat and organized?

Yes   No   **7.** Can you follow directions well?

Yes   No   **8.** Do you have an interest in human biology and anatomy?

Yes   No   **9.** Are you sensitive to the needs of other people?

Yes   No   **10.** Do you not mind working weekends and evenings?

If you answered "Yes" to most of these questions, you have what it takes to make a good funeral attendant. Read on to learn more about this job.

## Let's Talk Money

Funeral attendants averaged $19,720 a year in 2005. The highest-paid funeral attendants earned over $32,000 a year. The hourly wage for this job ranges from $7 to $16.

## *What* You'll Do

As a funeral attendant, you'll help a funeral director manage funerals, cremation services, and general business. Your duties will include basic housekeeping duties: Washing limousines and hearses, cleaning rooms, and setting up and putting away tables, chairs, urns, vases, candles, and other items used during visitations and services. You will have to keep the visitation rooms and possibly a chapel looking nice, decorating them with flowers and polishing the furniture. You may assist the funeral director with paperwork, preparing obituary notices or applying for death certificates. Much of this work is now done online.

Funeral attendants spend lots of time around the dead. You may pick up bodies at the hospital morgue or from nursing homes. You'll have to help lift bodies to move them around—from a hospital bed to a stretcher, for instance, or from an embalming table into a coffin or casket. If a body must wait more than 24 hours between death and burial, it must be embalmed or refrigerated; you'll wheel bodies in and out of a giant refrigerator on their way to the embalming room or cremation chamber. You may handle the bodies yourself, cleaning them with warm water and soap, and helping the embalmer prepare them properly. You may dress bodies and put them into their coffins. You may be in charge of funeral equipment such as stretchers and lowering straps (used to lower coffins into graves).

Today more than one-fourth of the deceased are cremated. You may likely help cremate bodies, placing them in a casket or container that is then put in a cremation chamber, an oven that reaches temperatures of 1,400°F to 1,800°F. After the ashes cool, you'll carefully remove them and place them in a container for the family; some families save the ashes in an urn, while others scatter them in some symbolic location.

## *Let's Talk Trends*

In 2005, there were slightly more than 30,000 funeral attendants working in the United States. The field isn't growing rapidly, but on the other hand, job-hunters aren't clamoring for line of work. Women now make up about half the graduates in this once male-dominated field.

As a funeral attendant, you'll see lots of grieving people. You'll speak to them kindly and make their difficult time a little bit easier. You may help them choose caskets or urns and plan funeral services for their loved ones. You'll help older people in and out of limousines and walk them to chairs in the visitation room. You may find family members crying on your shoulder.

## *Who* You'll Work For

★ A smaller family-owned funeral home
★ A larger "regional partner" funeral home

## *Where* You'll Work

You'll do most of your work in the funeral home. Some of your day will be spent in visitation rooms and chapels; you'll have to dress somewhat formally and speak in a quiet, polite voice when mourners are present. You may spend time in the embalming room. That's where the embalmer prepares the body for view and burial or cremation, for instance, by replacing bodily fluids with embalming fluid to prevent rapid decomposition. You'll wear protective clothing and gloves to keep fluids from touching your body when you touch the dead person. The smells can sometimes be strong—you'd better have an iron stomach. You may also enter the funeral home's giant refrigerator where it stores un-embalmed bodies or the room that houses its cremation chamber.

Your work may take you beyond the confines of the funeral home. You may drive a hearse to pick up bodies from the hospital morgue or to deliver bodies to the cemetery. Sometimes families want to hold funerals at synagogues, other houses of worship, or personally meaningful sites. You'll spend some of your time at cemeteries, helping to carry coffins as a pallbearer or standing quietly to show your respect during funerals and memorial services.

## Your Typical Day

Here are the highlights of a typical day for a funeral attendant.

✓ **Hold a morning conference.** You greet pair of customers: a woman whose elderly husband has died and their daughter. You first show them into the casket display room so they can see the available caskets. You then escort them into the funeral director's office and sit down as they convey their requests to the funeral director. The deceased was a Korean War veteran who liked 1950s rock and roll music; the director asks you to assemble a playlist of his favorite songs to play during the service.

✓ **Prepare the deceased.** After the customers leave, you and the funeral director begin a cremation, placing a body in the cremation chamber. Later that morning, you help the embalmer prepare a body, cleaning it, helping embalm, dressing the person and laying him in the casket. The cremation is now finished; you remove the remains from the cremation chamber and place them in an urn.

✓ **Set up for viewing.** You sweep and vacuum the viewing room and set up chairs for a visitation. You wheel in the casket and open the lid to reveal the deceased. You arrange flowers and personal items from the deceased on and around the casket and turn on music. When guests start arriving, you greet them at the door and show them in.

## What You Can Do Now

✴ Take classes in biology and chemistry.
✴ Take a psychology class to understand how people sort through their emotions.
✴ Practice being a good listener.
✴ Practice good manners and courteous public speaking.
✴ Find a summer job or internship in a funeral home.
✴ Volunteer at a nursing home—you'll be around lots of old people and will see how family members react when someone dies.

# *What Training You'll Need*

Before you become a full-time funeral attendant, you'll probably want to graduate from high school (a high school diploma isn't necessary, but is recommended) and to have a driver's license. Depending on your state, you may need to be trained in how to handle blood and avoid catching diseases from dead bodies. Your prospective employer will probably run a criminal background check on you. Some states require funeral directors to pay a fee to register each funeral attendant working for them as licensed funeral attendants. However, in most cases a license is not necessary, and as a funeral attendant you will not be required to register yourself. The registration requirements are meant to ensure that all funeral attendants are properly supervised. Check out the National Funeral Directors Association Web site for information on licensing requirements for funeral workers in each state.

Much of the work you'll do as a funeral attendant is a matter of common sense, and you can gain the specific training you need on the job. At work, you'll also study the various types and costs of coffins and urns and learn how to help mourners choose them. You may learn how to drive a hearse or van. You'll learn how to move a dead body from place to place, how to open and close coffins at appropriate points in a service, and how to get coffins into graves or crypts by using lifts or straps. You may learn how to cremate bodies and handle the ashes. You'll learn how to prepare a grave and graveside for a funeral. Your employer may teach you how to speak to mourners and how to help them in and out of limousines. He or she will also teach you how to prepare viewing rooms and chapels, setting up chairs and placing candles and flowers. You need to know how to sweep, vacuum, and mop, and how to dust and polish furniture. You may learn the basics of arranging flowers for funeral services.

# *How to Find a Job*

Look for advertisements in the local newspaper or on the Internet. You can find local opportunities by doing an Internet search for "funeral attendant" or "mortuary assistant" plus your hometown. You can also look on job search Web sites such as Monster.com. One of the best ways to find a job as a funeral attendant is to go to a funeral home and offer your services. Often jobs are not advertised, but a funeral director may be happy to hire a good worker. Bring your high school transcript and a résumé that includes information about any

# The Inside Scoop: Q&A

**Randy William Clark**
**Certified funeral attendant**
**Baileyville, Maine**

**Q:** *How did you get your job?*

**A:** After I delivered eulogies and served as a pall-bearer at some friends' funerals, a local funeral director mentioned the fact that I seemed relatively comfortable working with the deceased's family members as well as the deceased. He asked me if I'd ever considered becoming a licensed funeral attendant and working part-time for him. So, that's exactly what I did and have really enjoyed it.

**Q:** *What do you like best about your job?*

**A:** Lots! There are so many myths out there about working with the dead and all sorts of horrible and terrible things going on during the preparation process. I enjoy clarifying those rumors. I like to explain that deceased folks are treated with respect and love while being prepared for viewing, cremation, or whatever the circumstance might be. For example, I massage the head and hands of the person being embalmed to re-circulate and stimulate color and bring back appearance as best as can be expected. I always think of the person being someone I love and care about.

**Q:** *What's the most challenging part of your job?*

**A:** It's so tough to see people in [emotional] pain. It's hard not show your own feelings when a parent has lost a child or anyone for that matter. There never is a right or correct thing to say to make someone feel better. Sometimes just to be there with a great set of ears and an ever-ready hug is a part of what folks need.

**Q:** *What are the keys to success to being a funeral attendant?*

**A:** Flexibility. It's tough to be ready at a minute's notice. The director might call me at two in the morning. Within a minute's notice I must be dressed in my suit, presentable, and ready to claim a body at a hospital, enter the scene of a suicide, or retrieve the remains of a car accident victim. Composure is a must.

jobs you've had. Dress conservatively and be on your best behavior. Remember the funeral director will want to know how you'll act around mourners. If the funeral director schedules an interview with you, show up on time. Impress the director with your enthusiasm, responsibility, and dignity.

Often attendants start working for funeral homes part-time in high school. If you're still in high school, this might be a good way to find out if a career in funeral services would suit you.

## *How to Talk Like a Pro*

Here are some terms you hear working as a funeral attendant:

* **Cremate** To burn a dead body. Cremation turns the body into ashes, which can then be collected and stored in a decorative container (an urn) or scattered in some symbolic place.
* **Hearse** A large car that carries coffins to and from funerals.
* **Mortuary science** The study of funerals, including embalming techniques, human physiology, cremation, state laws, and grief counseling. You can study for such a program at college or at a private mortuary school.

## *Secrets for Success*

See the following suggestions and turn to the appendix for advice on résumés and interviews.

* According to the National Funeral Directors Association (NFDA), families nowadays want personalized funerals that celebrate the individuality of the deceased. You'll be a valuable asset if you can help customize a service, such as by preparing Webcasts of services, or putting together a slide show of the key moments in the person's life to be shown during the funeral.
* Funerals are time-sensitive, and you need to be very well informed about your own use of time. Did you place a timely call for flowers or any catering needs? If you tell someone you can perform a certain task with the body of the deceased in certain amount of time, you need to be able to do it—or keep your supervisor posted as to any complications.

# *Reality Check*

It's hard to be around death every day. As a funeral attendant, you'll see the bodies of people who have died in gruesome ways, and you'll hear the stories of people who have died tragically. You'll have to learn how to handle the emotions that will arise from your work. Funeral workers do sometimes break down and cry, but the best ones manage to keep the tears back until the mourners have left.

# *Some Other Jobs to Think About*

★ Cosmetologist. Though most cosmetologists work on living people, a few work for funeral homes helping to prepare the dead for viewing during a funeral. In addition to applying makeup, you might also fix the hair of the dead.

★ Floral designer. If you like flowers but don't like funerals, become a floral designer. You'll spend your days arranging flowers—sometimes for funerals, but also for happy occasions like weddings and proms.

★ EMT or paramedic. If you have a strong stomach and want to help people, but yearn for more action than you may see as a funeral home attendant, consider a career as an emergency medical technician or paramedic.

# *How You Can Move Up*

★ Become an embalmer. You'll prepare bodies for burial by replacing their body fluids with embalming fluid. You'll need to study embalming at mortuary school or college and pass an exam to get certified.

★ Become a funeral director. If you earn a college degree (bachelor's or associate's) in mortuary science, serve a one-year apprenticeship, and pass a state licensing exam (these requirements vary somewhat by state), you can manage a funeral home.

★ Become a social worker. This isn't directly related to funeral work, but social workers handle many of the same emotional situations that funeral attendants encounter—death, dying, and grieving survivors.

## Web Sites to Surf

**American Society of Embalmers.** This site has lots of information about working in the funeral industry, and of course, about embalming.
http://www.amsocembalmers.org

**National Funeral Directors Association.** This is the largest association of funeral directors in the country.   http://www.nfda.org

Make occasions beautiful

# Floral Designer

Spend your days surrounded by flowers

Display and sell your artistic vision

Great Careers

# *Floral* Designer

Does spending your time around flowers sound like a dream come true? If you become a floral designer, this could be your reality. Everyone needs flowers for special events such as weddings, funerals, and proms, and many businesses like to have floral arrangements on hand as decoration, so there's steady work for florists in towns of all sizes. Many people are attracted to floral design because it gives them a chance to create beautiful displays. Florists can be artists as well as craftspeople. The pay can be decent, too. Becoming a proficient floral designer does take some training, either on the job or at a floral design school, but it's possible to become an accomplished florist within a year of finishing high school.

## *Is This Job for You?*

To find out if being a floral designer is right for you, read each of the following questions and answer "Yes" or "No."

| | | | |
|---|---|---|---|
| Yes | No | **1.** | Do you like being around flowers and greenery? |
| Yes | No | **2.** | Are you free from allergies to pollen and dust? |
| Yes | No | **3.** | Do you like to work with your hands? |
| Yes | No | **4.** | Do you like weddings? |
| Yes | No | **5.** | Do you have a sense of color, style, and space? |
| Yes | No | **6.** | Can you come up with ideas for floral designs? |
| Yes | No | **7.** | Are you interested in learning the names and decorative qualities of plants and flowers? |
| Yes | No | **8.** | Are you outgoing and polite? |
| Yes | No | **9.** | Can you work independently? |
| Yes | No | **10.** | Would you enjoy traveling to different locations to set up arrangements? |

If you answered "Yes" to most of these questions, you may have the talent to pursue a career as a floral designer. To find out more about this job, read on.

## *What* You'll Do

As a floral designer, you'll order flowers from one or more wholesalers for your shop or business and take care of the blossoms when they

## Let's Talk Money

The average floral designer makes $21,060 a year, according to 2006 data from the U.S. Bureau of Labor Statistics. The highest paid designers average nearly $33,000 annually. Hourly wages range from $7 to $16 an hour.

arrive. To do this, you'll condition them and store them properly. You'll have to keep your shop and work area clean and make sure your tools are all in good condition.

You'll spend lots of your time arranging flowers. You'll make bouquets, corsages, and tabletop arrangements of all kinds. You'll use scissors and knives to cut stems; you'll have to be careful to avoid cutting yourself or straining your wrists and hands. You'll stick flowers into floral foam and enhance them with greens and ribbons. Some of the arrangements you make will be for your store, if you have one. They'll impress customers who walk in, and you might even be able to sell them on the spot.

Sometimes customers will pick up their flowers; other times you'll deliver them and see that they're set up properly. You may develop your upper body strength if you have to carry heavy arrangements. You may have to return to wedding or funeral sites to retrieve your containers after the events are finished. You'll need excellent customer-service manners. You'll communicate with customers all the time, in person, on the phone, and by e-mail. You'll discuss their floral needs and help them choose appropriate designs. If they order flowers to be sent to someone in another state or country, you'll help them make the order and then send it on to a distance delivery service such as FTD.

## *Who* You'll Work For

- ✻ An independent flower shop
- ✻ An Internet floral business
- ✻ A grocery store's floral department
- ✻ A caterer
- ✻ An interior designer
- ✻ A flower wholesaler
- ✻ Yourself

## Let's Talk Trends

Job opportunities for floral designers are expected to grow as fast as the average of all occupations through 2014, according to the Bureau of Labor Statistics. Floral sales have been increasing lately among both businesses and homeowners. Internet floral shops and grocery stores should have lots of jobs, while positions at traditional small flower shops will decline.

# *Where You'll Work*

Many businesses sell flowers. Most florists used to work in stand-alone floral shops, and these still exist. You may be able to find at job at a floral shop. If you do, your surroundings will probably be attractive and filled entirely with flowers. Customers who walk in will immediately notice the yellow daffodils, blue irises, spiky birds of paradise, colorful roses, graceful calla lilies, and all the other flowers sold there. You'll help decorate the shop with arrangements designed to impress walk-in customers with the quality of the work and flowers available there.

You're more likely to find a job at a grocery store's floral department or at an Internet floral business, both of which are becoming more common than independent flower shops. If you work at a grocery store, you'll probably be in a floral department that's open to the rest of the store. Your customers may come to the store just to buy flowers, but they may also be shopping for groceries as well. The surroundings won't be as attractive as those in a florist shop, but they will be convenient if you need to do some shopping of your own! If you work at an Internet florist, you may never see customers. Instead you'll be in a large facility equipped with refrigerators and work tables, and all of your work will be shipped to customers, many of them in other states.

Many florists work in their own homes. If you decide to go into business for yourself, you could do the same thing, perhaps specializing in one type of flower arrangement, such as wedding flowers. Most florists make some trips to homes, businesses, or churches to deliver or set up flowers.

# Your Typical Day

Here are the highlights of a typical Saturday for a floral designer.

✓ **Prepare in the morning.** You receive a shipment of fresh flowers from a wholesale company, condition them, and place them in the refrigerators. You then make several arrangements for a wedding: seven bowls of lilies and ferns for the tables at the reception, a basket of lily of the valley for the flower girl, bouquets of iris tied with gold ribbon for the bridesmaids, and a gorgeous, cascading crescent of white roses for the bride. You set aside some white orchids to place on the wedding cake.

✓ **Greet customers.** You clean up the flower arranging area and then greet several customers who arrive in the middle of the day. You help a young man choose a corsage for a prom and assist a daughter in choosing flowers for her father's funeral.

✓ **Deliver wedding flowers.** In the afternoon you load the wedding arrangements into the van and drive first to the church, where you decorate the altar and leave the bouquets in the refrigerator. You then drive to the reception hall, where you place arrangements on the tables and decorate the wedding cake.

# What You Can Do Now

✴ Practice arranging flowers at home.
✴ Study the names of flowers.
✴ Look closely at floral arrangements that you see in businesses or in magazines.
✴ Visit florists' shops to see what sort of arrangements are popular.
✴ Read books on floral design.
✴ Take art classes, especially develop your color sense.
✴ Get a part-time or summer job that involves dealing with customers to practice your customer service skills.
✴ Find an internship at a florist or flower shop.

# What Training You'll Need

You don't necessarily need any training to get a job at a florist shop, but some training can certainly help. Many florists hire assistants right out of high school with no floral training, and train them on the job. If you're reliable, creative, and willing to work up from the bottom, you can become a professional florist simply by working in the field.

Even if you do get a job as a floral designer right out of high school, you'll probably want to take some training courses. Your local community college may offer classes or a certificate program in floral design. Some flower shops also offer classes in floral design, and there are numerous private floral design schools. You can find these by searching the Internet or looking in the Yellow Pages. Many professional florists believe that the best way to learn floral design is to take a full course of study at a dedicated floral school, because taking single classes here and there won't teach you the full range of floral skills you may need. A full course in basic floral design can take anywhere from five weeks to six months, depending on the schedule, and can include both basic and advanced techniques. These might include quaint Victorian-style bouquets such as the "tussie-mussie," minimalist Japanese arrangements, centerpieces that can incorporate over 20 different types of flowers and cover most of a table, and all sorts of corsages and hand-held bouquets. You should finish a course able to design and create arrangements completely on your own, with no help from a shop supervisor. (One bonus of taking floral design courses is that you may get to bring home the arrangements you make in class!)

You can start with basic floral design and then branch into specialties such as wedding design, funeral design, wearable flowers, and table arrangements. You may study European design techniques, the use of balloons in arrangements, and tropical plants. There aren't many formal certifications in this field, but American Institute of Floral Designers offers an accreditation examination for florists who want to prove their ability in several different categories of floral design.

## *How to Talk Like a Pro*

Here are a few terms you may hear as a floral designer:

- **FTD, Teleflora, and American Floral Services** These are all services that enable customers to buy flowers in one place and have them delivered to a recipient far away.
- **Floral foam** A firm foam used to hold stems in a floral arrangement.
- **Floristry** The art of arranging flowers; floral design.
- **Horticulture** The study or practice of growing plants in a garden.
- **Ikebana** The Japanese style of elegant flower arranging.

# The Inside Scoop: Q&A

**Holly Kromer**
**Floral designer**
**Wooster, Ohio**

**Q:** *How did you get your job?*

**A:** I began working at the shop as a floral designer intern. I did my internship with them and I have continued to work there ever since.

**Q:** *What do you like best about your job?*

**A:** No two days are ever alike in the floral shop. Every day I get to do different designs with different flower choices and colors. Even when I'm taking orders for customers, I'm helping them make great decisions about flower designs, flower choices, or which color is best for the occasion. What I like best is being creative. My boss is always willing to see my new ideas, and she likes that I have a modern look to all my designs.

**Q:** *What's the most challenging part of your job?*

**A:** Learning everything that there is to know in the floral industry. It's not just flowers, there are a lot of small elements required to make it all flow well and keep customers happy and coming back. You have to have a large supply of different containers, baskets and vases on hand. When you run out of certain supplies and don't have time to get more, you need to find a quick solution.

**Q:** *What are the keys to success to being a floral designer?*

**A:** Being able to think quickly and be quick on your feet. Floral work can be very fast paced and sometimes if the customer does not like a design you need to think quickly and help them find a solution that works best for both of you.

## How to Find a Job

There are several places to look for jobs. Read the classified advertisements in your local paper. Do an Internet search for "floral designer" plus your hometown. Search for "floral designer" at a job search Web site such as Monster.com. Check out the job listings on professional Web sites, such as the one for the American Institute of Floral Designers. You can also go in person to flower shops and offer your services. Often businesses will hire employees even if they haven't advertised a job. Floral design schools sometimes help graduates find jobs—if you decide to pay for a training program, look for one with a good job placement service.

Many employers want to find experienced floral designers, but they may offer you a job as a cashier or delivery person; this is a great way to learn floral design on the job. If you've taken high school classes on floral design, bring photographs of your work to show to prospective employers. When you go to an interview, be sure to show up on time. Your boss will want to know that you won't come late to work. Dress nicely and be polite. Show the prospective employer that you're enthusiastic about floral design, and that you'd be pleasant to have working in the shop.

## Secrets for Success

See the following suggestions and turn to the appendix for advice on résumés and interviews.

* Please your customers. People want to buy flowers from someone who is friendly, courteous, and always delivers a quality product on time.
* Learn what takes how long in your work—your big days are deadline-oriented, and you don't want to be perfecting your first centerpiece when the bride's sister arrives to pick up all ten!

## Reality Check

Flowers have to be arranged at the last possible minute so they'll be fresh. That means lots of work on holidays and weekends when most big events and weddings occur.

## Some Other Jobs to Think About

* **Gardener.** If you like flowers but also enjoy making plants grow, you might enjoy working as a gardener, either maintaining gardens for homes or businesses or tending plants at a plant nursery.

- ✻ **Wedding planner.** If you like weddings, you can get into planning all the details, including flowers. There are lots of schools providing specialized training in this area.
- ✻ **Funeral attendant.** You'd help set up and run funerals at a funeral home; this would include arranging flowers around the chapel or visitation room.

## *How You Can Move Up*

- ✻ Become a head floral designer. As head florist, you'd manage a flower shop and train assistants. You'll need some experience in accounting and business management. As a head floral designer, you may oversee the design or junior florists.
- ✻ Open your own floral shop. If you go this route, take the time to learn basic business skills, including accounting; owning a business can be risky, and you don't want to lose your investment.
- ✻ Become an interior designer. If you enjoy design, you might like designing the insides of rooms, picking paint or wallpaper, furniture, and decorations. You'll need a college degree to get into this competitive field.
- ✻ Become a landscape architect or horticulturist. You'd plan the overall landscaping for homes and businesses, including gardens, electricity, and drainage systems. Floral design experience will help you get ahead, though you'll also need a bachelor's degree.

### *Web Sites to Surf*

**American Institute of Floral Designers.** This organization is dedicated to promoting floral design as a professional career. The Web site displays educational and job opportunities and notices of regular meetings for professional florists.  http://www.aifd.org

**Floral Design Institute.** This floral design school (one of many easily found on the Internet) offers several classes in floral design, including a distance learning program for students who can't attend its classes in person. http://www.floraldesigninstitute.com

Make custom clothing

# Seamstress, Tailor, Upholsterer

Make old fabric-covered furniture look like new

Alter clothes to fit perfectly

# Seamstress, Tailor, Upholsterer

Do you love the look and feel of fabric? Does the construction of clothing or fabric-covered furniture interest you? Do you like the smell of new car seats? And are you good with your hands? If so, you should consider a career in one of the sewing professions. Seamstresses and tailors make custom clothing and perform alterations to make off-the-rack clothes fit perfectly. Upholsterers sew cloth and leather covers for furniture and car seats and install them on top of springs and cushioning. Though in general the sewing professions are in something of a decline, shows like *Project Runway* are capturing a huge audience, and with new custom-pattern software making custom clothing more available to ordinary people, interest in jobs related to clothing design appear to be resurging. There's definitely a demand for people with the skill to make custom clothing and furniture.

## Is This Job for You?

To find out if being a tailor, seamstress, or upholsterer is right for you, read each of the following questions and answer "Yes" or "No."

Yes No **1.** Do you like working with your hands?

Yes No **2.** Do you have good manual dexterity?

Yes No **3.** Are you strong (for upholsterers)?

Yes No **4.** Can you sit still for hours?

Yes No **5.** Do you have good eyesight?

Yes No **6.** Do you like to look at and handle cloth?

Yes No **7.** Do you like to look at clothing or furniture?

Yes No **8.** Can you work independently?

Yes No **9.** Can you measure things precisely?

Yes No **10.** Are you a perfectionist?

If you answered "Yes" to most of these questions, you may have the talent to pursue a career as a seamstress, tailor, or upholsterer. To find out more about these jobs, read on.

## What You'll Do

If you become a seamstress or tailor, you'll make and repair clothing for customers. Tailors are generally thought of as being male and making clothing for men, and seamstresses or dressmakers are typically

## Let's Talk Money

The average income for tailors, dressmakers, and custom sewers is about $23,000 per year, according to the U.S. Bureau of Labor Statistics. The highest earners made around $36,000 a year. Upholsterers earned an average income of about $28,000, though the highest-paid earned nearly $42,000.

female and mostly create clothing for women. However, the difference today is becoming irrelevant. Sometimes men who sew for a living are called "seamsters." As a tailor or seamstress, much of your work will be alterations of off-the-rack garments. You'll do some of the alterations by hand and some with a sewing machine. Some customers will want you to sew new garments for them using lengths of fabric and patterns. You may even create your own patterns and garment designs, either by hand or by using new computer programs that generate patterns based on your clients' measurements. Some seamstresses and tailors specialize in costumes for theaters and film studios. Others make items such as custom curtains.

Seamstresses and tailors are considered custom sewers. Another type of sewing worker works in a factory; in larger factories they may work as sewing machine operators, textile cutting machine setters, or pattern makers. The pay can be about the same, but if you work in a factory, you'll be making large numbers of the same mass-produced garments instead of custom garments.

As an upholsterer, you'll make and repair furniture that is covered with fabric and padding. You may also upholster car seats in leather or cloth. To make a new piece of furniture, you'll start with a wooden frame (probably made by someone else). You'll stretch webbing over it, tack it down tight, and attach springs. You'll cover the springs with padding or stuffing to make a soft surface. You'll then cut out pieces of fabric, sew them together, and glue or tack them over the padding. You may add decorations such as ribbon or buttons. To fix furniture, you'll rip out old fabric and stuffing, re-glue the frame where it has come loose, and replace any portions of the webbing and springs that have worn out. Then you'll cover the springs with padding and the cloth covers you have cut and sewn together. You may help customers choose fabric based on pattern, texture, and price. You may deliver finished pieces to your customers. You may upholster car interiors, in addition to furniture.

## *Who You'll Work For*

✯ A clothing store
✯ An alterations shop
✯ A costume shop
✯ A theater
✯ A fashion or apparel designer
✯ A dry cleaner
✯ A furniture store
✯ A furniture repair shop
✯ An automobile upholstery shop
✯ Yourself

## *Where You'll Work*

As a tailor or seamstress, you may work in an alterations shop or in the alterations department of a clothing store. You'll do your work sitting at a table that contains your sewing machine, needles and thread, pins, scissors, measuring tape, and other pieces of equipment. When you fit clothes on customers, you'll have them stand on a raised box in front of a mirror. This gives you access to their feet and allows them to see how the garments look on them.

As an upholsterer, you may work in a furniture factory or a furniture repair shop. You'll work in a room that has enough space to store and manipulate big pieces of furniture such as couches, and possibly bolts of fabric. You may do some work in a garage that can hold vehicles. You'll probably do some of your work sitting or squatting on the floor, and sometimes you'll have to stand up for long periods of time. You may spend some of your time in a delivery van,

### *Let's Talk Trends*

In 2004 in the United States, about 85,000 people worked as tailors or dressmakers; more than half of them were self-employed. About 53,000 worked as upholsterers; 27 percent of them were self-employed. The number of positions in both fields has been declining, but some experts predict that given the do-it-yourself craze, the increased popularity of fashion design may create a resurgence in the field.

picking up and dropping off pieces of furniture. Many upholsterers, tailors, and seamstresses work at home. Of course, you'll need a room big enough to hold your sewing or upholstering equipment.

# Your Typical Day

Here are highlights of a typical day for a seamstress.

✓ **Mark for alterations.** A high school student comes in with several cheerleading uniforms that she inherited from a classmate who has graduated. The uniforms are much too big for their current owner. You fold and pin them so that they'll fit properly and tell her to pick them up in a week.

✓ **Bead a wedding dress.** A client wants the hem of her wedding dress decorated with rhinestones and pearls. You spend two hours working on this but don't finish. This job will take several days to complete.

✓ **Make a cape.** Another client has brought you a pattern and fabric to make a cape for her son's Halloween costume. You lay the cloth out on the pattern, cut out the pieces, and quickly run them together on your sewing machine.

# What You Can Do Now

✴ Take art classes. Learn about line and color. Practice drawing.

✴ Take classes in sewing or upholstery.

✴ Practice sewing: Hem or alter your clothes, or sew your own clothes from patterns. Try to stitch both by hand and on your machine.

✴ Examine the construction of your own clothes and of clothes in stores to learn about quality.

✴ Visit fabric stores to examine fabrics.

✴ Do the laundry and see what it does to clothes.

# What Training You'll Need

Custom sewing and upholstery are both skilled trades that require a great deal of training to master. You'll have to learn how to take measurements, cut cloth to a pattern, and sew both by hand and by machine. You'll also need to understand the properties of various kinds of cloth. You don't need any particular certification or license to

# The Inside Scoop: Q&A

**Wally Nicholson**
**Upholsterer**
**Vadnais Heights, Minnesota**

**Q:** *How did you get your job?*

**A:** I put myself through upholstery school at night while I was working for a local furniture store. I started out on my own doing part-time work for extra income. After one-and-a-half years I went full time. I've been self-employed since 1993. I'm going stronger than ever.

**Q:** *What do you like best about your job?*

**A:** I like making people's dreams come true and seeing their ideas brought to life by doing things like upholstering family heirlooms or building a custom street rod interior from scratch. It is rewarding to be able to do this work for a living.

**Q:** *What's the most challenging part of your job?*

**A:** Working with the various personalities of customers can be very challenging. Getting the work done on time is also hard, as you never know exactly how long something will take until you are halfway through it.

**Q:** *What are the keys to success to being an upholsterer?*

**A:** Quality is of the utmost to being successful in this field—not just meeting the customer's expectations but exceeding them. You have to be able to estimate jobs accurately and be well-organized.

enter a sewing field, but you will have to spend a lot of time learning your trade.

If you want to become an upholsterer, you can expect to spend several years learning your skills. Most upholsterers learn the trade on the job, working as assistants in upholstery shops. You might be able to find an upholsterer to take you on as an apprentice; if you do this, be sure to work out the details of the apprenticeship before you sign a contract. The same applies to dressmaking and tailoring. Most people learn their skills on the job. Many sewing professionals first learned to sew at home with family members. Others train as apprentices or assistants in shops.

If you want to advance, it's a good idea to have some formal training. Your high school may offer classes in sewing or upholstery. Some community and technical colleges offer certification programs in dressmaking, tailoring, and furniture or automotive upholstery; some automotive upholstery programs include training in glass repair as well. An Internet search for your hometown plus "upholstery program" or "upholstery certification" can locate upholstery programs. For custom sewing, search for "dressmaking training" or "tailoring." You can also call technical colleges in your area to ask about programs. Training programs cover fibers, fabrics, cutting cloth, altering patterns, and finishing work. A certification or associate's degree in the field will make you more marketable because employers will see that you already know basic skills. However you start, you should expect to spend years mastering your craft. You can learn enough to do basic upholstery and simple custom sewing in a few weeks, but it can take 8 to 10 years to learn how to do the finest custom work.

## *How to Talk Like a Pro*

Here are a few words you'll hear as a seamstress, tailor, or upholsterer:

- ✦ **Garment** An item of clothing. The field of clothing manufacture is also called the "garment industry."
- ✦ **Interfacing** A layer of cloth sewn inside the main fabric of a garment to help support the garment in a high-stress area, such as a collar or waistband.
- ✦ **Seam** A line of stitches that joins two pieces of fabric together.
- ✦ **Textile** A fabric; a cloth.
- ✦ **Welt pocket** A pocket with one or two "lips."

## *How to Find a Job*

Most businesses that hire seamstresses, tailors, or upholsterers want experienced workers who know at least the basics of the trade. You'll have a much easier time finding work if you already know how to sew or have begun to study upholstery. If you don't have any experience, however, don't let that stop you from looking for work because most workers in the sewing trades learn most of their craft on the job. It just may be harder for you to find a job, and your starting pay will probably be lower.

To find job opportunities, read the newspaper classified ads or conduct an Internet search for the name of your hometown plus "seamstress" or "upholsterer." You can also go directly to alteration shops, dry cleaners, furniture repair shops, or other places that hire seamstresses or upholsterers and offer your services. If you get an interview, be sure to show up on time! Be polite and enthusiastic, and dress neatly. Bring along a copy of your résumé. If you've already sewn some garments, bring them along to show your prospective employer.

## Secrets for Success

See the following suggestions and turn to the appendix for advice on résumés and interviews.

✳ Attention to detail is key. People are very picky about how their clothes look and fit or about the smoothness of their furniture or car seats. Take your time to do the job right.

✳ Learn how long it takes you to do specific tasks—putting the buttons on a shirt, hemming a dress, or taking in a jacket. You will learn what you need to do faster so that it pays to do the work, and you will also start being able to plan your work schedule.

## Reality Check

Work carefully to avoid injuries! Seamstresses and upholsterers get lots of aches and pains from bending over their work. Repetitive stress injuries such as carpal tunnel syndrome are common. And watch out for those sharp needles and scissors!

## Some Other Jobs to Think About

✳ Textile machine operator or tender. You'll work in a textile factory making fibers such as cotton, rayon, or fiberglass, and then transforming them into cloth on knitting or weaving machines.

✳ Sewing machine operator. You'll sew together the pieces of garments for a mass clothing manufacturer.

✫ Pattern maker. You'll work with a clothing designer to convert his or her designs into patterns of various sizes so that a factory can produce a large number of the same garment.

✫ Shoe or leather worker. You'll work in a factory or shoe repair shop assembling shoes and bags made of leather, canvas, or plastic.

✫ Clothing salesperson. You'll help customers choose clothing that fits well, and possibly mark new clothes for alteration.

✫ Drapery maker. You'll specialize in sewing drapes and creating window treatments for your clients.

# *How You Can Move Up*

✫ Become a shop supervisor. As a manager, you'll command a higher salary than a seamstress or upholsterer.

✫ Open your own shop. As a tailor, dressmaker, or custom upholsterer, running your own business will allow you to choose your jobs and earn more money. You should learn the basics of running a business before you try this.

✫ Become a fashion designer. You'll need to go to college to study fashion design, but a background in sewing is essential.

## *Web Sites to Surf*

**Livingsoft Northwest.** A site that sells custom patterns made to individual measurements. http://www.livingsoftnw.com

**Professional Association of Custom Clothiers.** This is an association of tailors, dressmakers, pattern makers, and various other sewing professionals. It has a list of schools that teach sewing and design skills. http://www.paccprofessionals.org

**Upholster Magazine Online.** This magazine publishes articles on upholstery, detailed instructions on upholstery techniques, and a discussion board on upholstery topics. http://www.upholster.com

Unlock your network

# Appendix A

Get your résumé ready

Ace your interview

# Putting Your Best Foot Forward

When 20-year-old Justin Schulman started job-hunting for a position as a fitness trainer—the first step toward managing a fitness facility—he didn't mess around. "I immediately opened the Yellow Pages and started calling every number listed under health and fitness, inquiring about available positions," he recalls. Schulman's energy and enterprise paid off: He wound up with interviews that led to several offers of part-time work.

Schulman's experience highlights an essential lesson for job seekers: There are plenty of opportunities out there, but jobs won't come to you—especially the career-oriented, well-paying ones that that you'll want to stick with over time. You've got to seek them out.

## Uncover Your Interests

Whether you're in high school or bringing home a full-time paycheck, the first step toward landing your ideal job is assessing your interests. You need to figure out what makes you tick. After all, there is a far greater chance that you'll enjoy and succeed in a career that taps into your passions, inclinations, and natural abilities. That's what happened with career-changer Scott Rolfe. He was already 26 when he realized he no longer wanted to work in the food industry. "I'm an avid outdoorsman," Rolfe says, "and I have an appreciation for natural resources that many people take for granted." Rolfe turned his passions into his ideal job as a forestry technician.

If you have a general idea of what your interests are, you're far ahead of the game. You may know that you're cut out for a health care career, for instance, or one in business. You can use a specific volume of Great Careers with a High School Diploma to discover what position to target. If you are unsure of your direction, check out the whole range of volumes to see the scope of jobs available.

You can also use interest inventories and skills-assessment programs to further pinpoint your ideal career. Your school or public librarian or guidance counselor should be able to help you locate such assessments. Web sites, such as America's Career InfoNet (http ://www.acinet.org) and Jobweb.com, also offer interest inventories.

You'll find suggestions for Web sites related to specific careers at the end of each chapter in any Great Careers with a High School Diploma volume.

## *Unlock Your Network*

The next stop toward landing the perfect job is networking. The word may make you cringe, but networking is simply introducing yourself and exchanging job-related and other information that may prove helpful to one or both of you. That's what Susan Tinker-Muller did. Quite a few years ago, she struck up a conversation with a fellow passenger on her commuter train. Little did she know that the natural interest she expressed in the woman's accounts payable department would lead to news about a job opening there. Tinker-Muller's networking landed her an entry-level position in accounts payable with MTV Networks. She is now the accounts payable administrator.

Tinker-Muller's experience illustrates why networking is so important. Fully 80 percent of openings are *never* advertised, and more than half of all employees land their jobs through networking, according to the U.S. Bureau of Labor Statistics. That's 8 out of 10 jobs that you'll miss if you don't get out there and talk with people. And don't think you can bypass face-to-face conversations by posting your résumé on job sites like Craigslist, Monster.com, and Hotjobs.com and then waiting for employers to contact you. That's so mid-1990s! Back then, tens of thousands, if not millions, of job seekers diligently posted their résumés on scores of sites. Then they sat back and waited . . . and waited . . . and waited. You get the idea. Big job sites have their place, of course, but relying solely on an Internet job search is about as effective throwing your résumé into a black hole.

Begin your networking efforts by making a list of people to talk to: teachers, classmates (and their parents), anyone you've worked with, neighbors, members of your church, synogogue, temple or mosque, and anyone you've interned or volunteered with. You can also expand your networking opportunities through the student sections of industry associations; attending or volunteering at industry events, association conferences, career fairs; and through job-shadowing. Keep in mind that only rarely will any of the people on your list be in a position to offer you a job. But whether they know it or not, they probably know someone who knows someone who is. That's why your networking goal is not to ask for a job but the name of someone to talk with. Even when you network with an employer, it's wise to say something like, "You may not have any positions available, but would you know someone I could talk with to find out more about what it's like to work in this field?"

Also, keep in mind that networking is a two-way street. For instance, you may be talking with someone who has a job opening that isn't appropriate for you. If you can refer someone else to the employer, either person may well be disposed to help you someday in the future.

# Dial-Up Help

Call your contacts directly, rather than e-mail them. (E-mails are too easy for busy people to ignore, even if they don't mean to.) Explain that you're a recent graduate; that Mr. Jones referred you; and that you're wondering if you could stop by for 10 or 15 minutes at your contact's convenience to find out a little more about how the industry works. If you leave this message as a voicemail, note that you'll call back in a few days to follow up. If you reach your contact directly, expect that they'll say they're too busy at the moment to see you. Ask, "Would you mind if I check back in a couple of weeks?" Then jot down a note in your date book or set up a reminder in your computer calendar and call back when it's time. (Repeat this above scenario as needed, until you get a meeting.)

Once you have arranged to talk with someone in person, prep yourself. Scour industry publications for insightful articles; having up-to-date knowledge about industry trends shows your networking contacts that you're dedicated and focused. Then pull together questions about specific employers and suggestions that will set you apart from the job-hunting pack in your field. The more specific your questions (for instance, about one type of certification versus another), the more likely your contact will see you as an "insider," worthy of passing along to a potential employer. At the end of any networking meeting, ask for the name of someone else who might be able to help you further target your search.

# Get a Lift

When you meet with a contact in person (as well as when you run into someone fleetingly), you need an "elevator speech." This is a summary of up to two minutes that introduces who you are, as well as your experience and goals. An elevator speech should be short enough to be delivered during an elevator ride with a potential employer from the ground level to a high floor. In it, it's helpful to show that 1) you know the business involved; 2) you know the company; 3) you're qualified (give your work and educational information); and 4) you're goal-oriented, dependable, and hardworking. You'll be surprised how much information you can include in two minutes. Practice this speech in front of a mirror until you have the key points down very well. It should sound natural though, and you should come across as friendly, confident, and assertive. Remember, good eye contact needs to be part of your presentation as well as your everyday approach when meeting prospective employers or leads.

## Get Your Résumé Ready

In addition to your elevator speech, another essential job-hunting tool is your résumé. Basically, a résumé is a little snapshot of you in words, reduced to one 8½ x 11-inch sheet of paper (or, at most, two sheets). You need a résumé whether you're in high school, college, or the workforce, and whether you've never held a job or have had many.

At the top of your résumé should be your heading. This is your name, address, phone numbers, and your e-mail address, which can be a sticking point. E-mail addresses such as sillygirl@yahoo.com or drinkingbuddy@hotmail.com won't score you any points. In fact they're a turn-off. So if you dreamed up your address after a night on the town, maybe it's time to upgrade. (And while we're on the subject, these days, potential employers often check Myspace pages, personal blogs, and Web sites. What's posted there has been known to cost candidates job offers.)

The first section of your résumé is a concise Job Objective: "Entry-level agribusiness sales representative seeking a position with a leading dairy cooperative." These days, with word-processing software, it's easy and smart to adapt your job objective to the position for which you're applying. An alternative way to start a résumé, which some recruiters prefer, is to rework the Job Objective into a Professional Summary. A Professional Summary doesn't mention the position you're seeking, but instead focuses on your job strengths: e.g., "Entry-level agribusiness sales rep; strengths include background in feed, fertilizer, and related markets and ability to contribute as a member of a sales team." Which is better? It's your call.

The body of a résumé typically starts with your Job Experience. This is a chronological list of the positions you've held (particularly the ones that will help you land the job you want). Remember: Never, never fudge anything. It is okay, however, to include volunteer positions and internships on the chronological list, as long as they're noted for what they are.

Next comes your Education section. Note: It's acceptable to flip the order of your Education and Job Experience sections if you're still in high school or don't have significant work experience. Summarize any courses you've taken in the job area you're targeting, any certifications you've achieved, relevant computer knowledge, special seminars, or other school-related experience that will distinguish you. Include your grade average if it's more than 3.0. Don't worry if you haven't finished your degree. Simply write that you're currently enrolled in your program (if you are).

In addition to these elements, other sections may include professional organizations you belong to and any work-related achievements, awards, or recognition you've received. Also, you can have a section for your interests, such as playing piano or soccer (and include any notable achievements regarding your interests, for instance, placed third in Midwest Regional Piano Competition). You should also note other special abilities, such as "Fluent in French," or "Designed own Web site." These sorts of activities will reflect well on you whether or not they are job-related.

You can either include your references or simply note, "References Upon Request." Be sure to ask your references permission to use their name, and alert them to the fact that they may be contacted, before you include them on your résumé. For more information on résumé writing, check out Web sites such as http://www.resume .monster.com.

# *Craft Your Cover Letter*

When you apply for a job either online or by mail, it's appropriate to include a cover letter. A cover letter lets you convey extra information about yourself than doesn't fit or isn't always appropriate in your résumé. For instance, in a cover letter, you can and should mention the name of anyone who referred you to the job. You can go into some detail about the reason you're a great match, given the job description. You can also address any questions that might be raised in the potential employer's mind (for instance, a gap in your résumé). Don't, however, ramble on. Your cover letter should stay focused on your goal: to offer a strong, positive impression of yourself and persuade the hiring manager that you're worth an interview. Your cover letter gives you a chance to stand out from the other applicants and sell yourself. In fact, 23 percent of hiring managers say a candidate's ability to relate his or her experience to the job at hand is a top hiring consideration, according to a CareerBuilder.com survey.

You can write a positive, yet concise cover letter in three paragraphs: An introduction containing the specifics of the job you're applying for; a summary of why you're a good fit for the position and what you can do for the company; and a closing with a request for an interview, your contact information, and thanks. Remember to vary the structure and tone of your cover letter. For instance, don't begin every sentence with "I."

# *Ace* Your Interview

Preparation is the key to acing any job interview. This starts with researching the company or organization you're interviewing with. Start with the firm, group, or agency's own Web site. Explore it thoroughly, read about their products and services, their history, and sales and marketing information. Check out their news releases, links that they provide, and read up on, or Google, members of the management team to get an idea of what they may be looking for in their employees.

Sites such as http://www.hoovers.com enable you to research companies across many industries. Trade publications in any industry (such as *Food Industry News*, *Hotel Business*, and *Hospitality Technology*) are also available at online or in hard copy at many college or public libraries. Don't forget to make a phone call to contacts you have in the organization to get a better idea of the company culture.

Preparation goes beyond research, however. It includes practicing answers to common interview questions:

- ✴ *Tell me about yourself.* Don't talk about your favorite bands or your personal history; give a brief summary of your background and interest in the particular job area.
- ✴ *Why do you want to work here?* Here's where your research into the company comes into play; talk about the firm's strengths and products or services.

✴ *Why should we hire you?* Now is your chance to sell yourself as a dependable, trustworthy, effective employee.

✴ *Why did you leave your last job?* Keep your answer short; never bad-mouth a previous employer. You can always say something simple, such as, "It wasn't a good fit, and I was ready for other opportunities."

Rehearse your answers, but don't try to memorize them. Responses that are natural and spontaneous come across better. Trying to memorize exactly what you want to say is likely to both trip you up and make you sound robotic.

As for the actual interview, to break the ice, offer a few pleasant remarks about the day, a photo in the interviewer's office, or something else similar. Then, once the interview gets going, listen closely and answer the questions you're asked, versus making any other point that you want to convey. If you're unsure whether your answer was adequate, simply ask, "Did that answer the question?" Show respect, good energy, and enthusiasm, and be upbeat. Employers are looking for workers who are enjoyable to be around, as well as good workers. Show that you have a positive attitude and can get along well with others by not bragging during the interview, overstating your experience, or giving the appearance of being too self-absorbed. Avoid one-word answers, but at the same time don't blather. If you're faced with a silence after giving your response, pause for a few seconds, and then ask, "Is there anything else you'd like me to add?" Never look at your watch and turn your cell phone off before an interview.

Near the interview's end, the interviewer is likely to ask you if you have any questions. Make sure that you have a few prepared, for instance:

✴ *"Tell me about the production process."*

✴ *"What's your biggest short-term challenge?"*

✴ *"How have recent business trends affected the company?"*

✴ *"Is there anything else that I can provide you with to help you make your decision?"*

✴ *"When will you make your hiring decision?"*

During a first interview, never ask questions like, "What's the pay?" "What are the benefits?" or "How much vacation time will I get?"

# *Find the Right Look*

Appropriate dress and grooming is also essential to interviewing success. For business jobs and many other occupations, it's appropriate to come to an interview in a nice (not stuffy) suit. However, different fields have various dress codes. In the music business, for instance, "business casual" reigns for many jobs. This is a slightly modified look, where slacks and a jacket are just fine for a man, and a nice skirt and blouse and jacket or sweater are acceptable for a woman. Dressing overly "cool" will usually backfire.

In general, tend to all the basics from shoes (no sneakers, sandals, or overly high heels) to outfits (no short skirts for women). Women should also avoid attention-getting necklines. Keep jewelry to a minimum. Tattoos and body jewelry are becoming more acceptable, but if you can take out piercings (other than a simple stud in your ear), you're better off. Similarly, unusual hairstyles or colors may bias an employer against you, rightly or wrongly. Make sure your hair is neat and acceptable (consider getting a haircut). Also go light on the makeup, self-tanning products, body scents, and other grooming agents. Don't wear a baseball cap or any other type of hat, and by all means, take off your sunglasses!

Beyond your physical appearance, you already know to be well bathed to minimize odor (leave your home early if you tend to sweat, so you can cool off in private), use a breath mint (especially if you smoke) make good eye contact, smile, speak clearly using proper English (or Spanish), use good posture (don't slouch), offer a firm handshake, and arrive within five minutes of your interview. (If you're unsure of where you're going, Mapquest or Google Map it and consider making a dry run to the site so you won't be late.) First impressions can make or break your interview.

# *Remember to Follow Up*

After your interview, send a thank-you note. This thoughtful gesture will separate you from most of the other candidates. It demonstrates your ability to follow through, and it catches your prospective employer's attention one more time. In a 2005 Careerbuilder.com survey, nearly 15 percent of 650 hiring managers said they wouldn't hire someone who failed to send a thank-you letter after the interview. Thirty-two percent say they would still consider the candidate, but would think less of him or her.

So do you hand write or e-mail the thank you letter? The fact is that format preferences vary. One in four hiring managers prefer to receive a thank-you note in e-mail form only; 19 percent want the e-mail, followed up with a hard copy; 21 percent want a typed hard-copy only, and 23 percent prefer just a handwritten note. (Try to check with an assistant on the format your potential employer prefers). Otherwise, sending an e-mail and a handwritten copy is a safe way to proceed.

## *Winning an Offer*

There are no sweeter words to a job hunter than, "We'd like to hire you." So naturally, when you hear them, you may be tempted to jump at the offer. *Don't.* Once an employer wants you, he or she will usually give you some time to make your decision and get any questions you may have answered. Now is the time to get specific about salary, benefits, and negotiate some of these points. If you haven't already done so, check out salary ranges for your position and area of the country on sites such as Payscale.com, Salary.com, and Salaryexpert.com (basic info is free; specific requests are not). Also find out what sort of benefits similar jobs offer. Then don't be afraid to negotiate in a diplomatic way. Asking for better terms is reasonable and expected. You may worry that asking the employer to bump up his or her offer may jeopardize your job, but handled intelligently, negotiating for yourself may in fact be a way to impress your future employer and get a better deal for yourself.

After you've done all the hard work that successful job-hunting requires, you may be tempted to put your initiative into autodrive. However, the efforts you made to land your job—from clear communication to enthusiasm—are necessary now to pave your way to continued success. As Danielle Little, a human-resources assistant, says, "You must be enthusiastic and take the initiative. There is an urgency to prove yourself and show that you are capable of performing any and all related tasks. If your manager notices that you have potential, you will be given additional responsibilities, which will help advance your career." So do your best work on the job, and build your credibility. Your payoff will be career advancement and increased earnings.

# Index